'DINOSAURS'
of the Deep
DISCOVER PREHISTORIC MARINE LIFE

'DINOSAURS'
of the Deep

DISCOVER PREHISTORIC MARINE LIFE

BY LARRY VERSTRAETE
PALEOART BY JULIUS CSOTONYI

TURNSTONE PRESS

'Dinosaurs' of the Deep: Discover Prehistoric Marine Life
Text Copyright © Larry Verstraete 2016
Paleoart Copyright © Julius Csotonyi 2016

Turnstone Press
Artspace Building
206–100 Arthur Street
Winnipeg, MB
R3B 1H3 Canada
www.TurnstonePress.com

Turnstone Press gratefully acknowledges the assistance of the Canada Council for the Arts, the Manitoba Arts Council, the Government of Canada through the Canada Book Fund, and the Province of Manitoba through the Book Publishing Tax Credit and the Book Publisher Marketing Assistance Program.

Turnstone Press also thanks the Canadian Fossil Discovery Centre (www.discoverfossils.com) in Morden, Manitoba, whose cooperation on this project was invaluable.

—

Design: Jamis Paulson
Paleontology Consultant: Victoria Markstrom
Photos, Maps, and Images: See page 76

Printed and bound in Canada by Friesens for Turnstone Press.

Library and Archives Canada Cataloguing in Publication

Verstraete, Larry, author
    'Dinosaurs' of the deep : discover prehistoric marine life
/ by Larry Verstraete ; paleoart by Julius Csotonyi.

Includes bibliographical references and index.
ISBN 978-0-88801-573-0 (hardback)

    1. Marine animals, Fossil--Juvenile literature. 2. Paleontology--Cretaceous--Juvenile literature. I. Csotonyi, Julius, 1973-, illustrator
II. Title.

QE766.V47 2016   j560'.457   C2016-903666-9

For my son, Stephen, and daughter, Ashley—once children, now adults, but still inspiring me every day.

TABLE OF CONTENTS

PREFACE

Years ago, I wrote an alphabet book about Manitoba. Having lived in Manitoba my entire life, I thought I knew my home province. I was wrong. I had much to learn.

Somewhere in my preliminary research, I encountered the word 'mosasaur'. Frequently mentioned as well was Bruce, the world's largest mosasaur, and the Canadian Fossil Discovery Centre, the museum in Morden, Manitoba where Bruce is on exhibit.

Although I knew that an ancient warm sea once covered much of the province, learning that creatures as large as dinosaurs once stalked prey in its waters was a revelation. I journeyed to Morden to view the monster myself and was not disappointed. With teeth the size of rail spikes and a body as long as two pick-up trucks, Bruce is fearsomely impressive.

And so began my fascination with the Western Interior Seaway and the life that flourished in it seventy million years ago. I discovered that although much had been written about dinosaurs and other land animals of the Cretaceous period, far less had been written about the Seaway and its creatures. When Turnstone Press and the Canadian Fossil Discovery Centre joined forces to fill the gap and were looking for a science writer for their project, I happily seized the opportunity.

The book is titled 'Dinosaurs' of the Deep and that deserves an explanation. In scientific circles, mosasaurs, plesiosaurs, ichthyosaurs, and other such sea creatures are classified as marine reptiles, not dinosaurs. Many dinosaurs have similar sounding names, however, like tyrannosaur, stegosaur, and brachiosaur. Perhaps because the root 'saur' (from the Latin saurus, meaning lizard) can be found in the names of so many creatures, we tend to lump them together. In many minds, the term 'dinosaur' covers a spectrum of exotic creatures that once thrived on land and in the seas of our planet, then died in a mysterious wave of extinction. Although not scientifically accurate, we've intentionally used 'dinosaurs' in the title to connect with readers, evoking a sense of the time, place, and fascination that is often associated with the word, then added the subtitle to clarify its content.

Paleontology is an ever-changing field. Each new discovery adds to our understandings about the past, but also fuels healthy debate when paleontologists weigh in with different interpretations of the evidence. To research the book, I tore into scientific papers, dipped into books and videos, scoured the Internet, visited dig sites, toured fossil museums and laboratories, and consulted experts more knowledgeable than me to obtain the most recent and most accurate information.

Many people came to my aid. At the top of a long list are three from the Canadian Fossil Discovery Centre. Peter Cantelon, Executive Director, and Trevor Frost, Administrative Director, welcomed me warmly and granted me access to the Centre's many resources. Victoria Markstrom, Field and Collection Manager, served as my anchor throughout the research process. Victoria toured me through the Centre's exhibits and its laboratory, answered my questions, accompanied me to an excavation site along the Manitoba Escarpment, combed through my drafts with a critical eye to ensure accuracy, and conferred with fellow scholars.

Morden resident Don Bell was also a great help. In paleontological circles, Don and fellow teacher, Henry Isaak, are genuine heroes, having braved many a cold night and long weekend in the 1970s retrieving and rescuing marine fossils that might otherwise have been destroyed along the Manitoba Escarpment. In interviews, Don shared his fossil hunting experiences and provided me with a greater understanding of the circumstances that ultimately led to the establishment of the Canadian Fossil Discovery Centre.

My research led me to many quarters and through detours along the way. On one memorable but busy day, while on a trip to the Netherlands, I convinced my wife to do a side tour of the Teylers Museum in Haarlem for a quick peek at one of its many treasures—the fossil remains of the first mosasaur ever discovered. Jo was remarkably patient, but then she knows me well. Once hooked on an idea, there's no letting go. The brief stop was especially fruitful. We struck up a conversation with the curator who informed us of two other world-famous fossils on display at the museum. One was *Archaeopteryx*, a half-bird, half-dinosaur creature that provided science with proof that the two were related. The other was a coelacanth, a fish thought to have been extinct until Marjorie Courtenay Latimer, a plucky museum curator in South Africa, spotted its blue fin among a catch of fish in 1938. All three discoveries rocked the world of science and challenged existing views about prehistoric life. Of course, I just had to write about them, and you'll find details about the three in this book.

It takes a team of professionals to produce a book of this caliber, and I was blessed with top notch supporters at Turnstone Press. From the start, this was a group effort and I am indebted to each of my talented and dedicated Turnstone partners as well as to paleoartist Julius Csotonyi whose stunning visuals help bring the text to life.

Behind my efforts stand others who have encouraged me over the years … friends, relatives and fellow writers … my wonderful and supportive family … my wife, Jo, who cheers me on daily. I couldn't have done this without all of you.

I started my research with many questions about the Western Interior Seaway and the creatures that dominated the prehistoric landscape. Writing the book fed my curiosity and partially satisfied my hunger to know more. I say 'partially' because like all subjects with open ends one question merely leads to another, fueling the quest to know even more. To me, that's what is so appealing about science, and paleontology in particular. There is still so much that we don't know, so much left to question, and in the case of paleontology, so many pages from the past that remain unscripted. A lifetime of wonder awaits whoever is curious enough to fill in the blanks.

—**Larry Verstraete**

'DINOSAURS'
of the Deep
DISCOVER PREHISTORIC MARINE LIFE

INTRODUCTION

Imagine that you are standing along the Trans-Canada Highway in southwestern Manitoba, or in a cornfield in central Kansas, or perhaps farther north in a pasture in Alberta. Look around. Check out your surroundings. Other than a few rolling hills and the occasional ridge or valley, the land around you is mostly flat. It seems to stretch all the way to the horizon. Kilometres of flatness with nothing much happening. Or so it seems.

Now peel away time. Go back seventy million years or more, to a period long before humans roamed Manitoba, Kansas, or Alberta, to a time known as the Cretaceous period. Imagine being in the same locations. The mostly flat land is under water, covered by a salty, warm sea. The air above, though breathable, swirls with sulfur and carbon dioxide, and other gases from nearby volcanoes.

There's nothing boring here. The ancient sea swarms with strange creatures. Six metre (13 feet) fish with mouthfuls of spiked teeth. Turtles the size of small cars. Giant squid 10 metres (33 feet) long. Lizard-like reptiles, some bigger than school buses, swish through the water, tails lashing while even sharks scoot away in fear.

The hunt is on. In the ancient sea, predators abound. Danger lurks everywhere. Survival is the key. One false move, one moment of distraction, could be the last for any prey.

Welcome to the Western Interior Seaway, a prehistoric sea filled with fierce creatures that once covered much of the Plains region of present-day Canada and the United States while dinosaurs roamed the land on both sides of it.

EVIDENCE OF OUR WATERY PAST

How do we know the Western Interior Seaway existed? How do we know marine reptiles flourished over Manitoba, Kansas, Alberta, and other regions?

Rocks tell part of the story, and geologists are their storytellers. Geologists are scientists who study the Earth and its formations. By charting the composition and distribution of rocks in different regions, geologists can tell much about the Earth's past (*see Three Types of Rock*).

In the Plains of North America, sedimentary rocks abound, indicating that at one time these regions were under water. Ridges, sand dunes, and steep slopes, known as escarpments, composed of sedimentary material border the Plains. They define the shorelines and beaches of the ancient Seaway. Higher elevations of igneous rocks flank both sides of the Plains, leading geologists to conclude that these were regions of volcanic activity, mountain-building, and frequent upheaval.

THREE TYPES OF ROCK

SEDIMENTARY—Rocks formed when deposits of sediment (sand, shells, bone fragments, etc.) that are transported by water, ice, or wind solidify together. Sedimentary rocks are often deposited in layers or strata, and frequently contain fossils. Sandstone is a type of sedimentary rock.

IGNEOUS—Rocks formed by the cooling and solidifying of volcanic material. Granite is a type of igneous rock.

METAMORPHIC—Rocks altered from their original state by intense heat and pressure. Gneiss is a type of metamorphic rock.

THE WESTERN INTERIOR SEAWAY

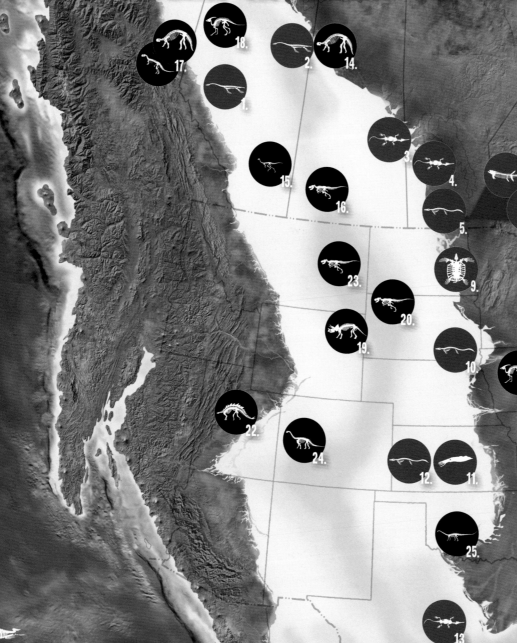

Fossils tell another side of the story. Paleontologists are scientists who find, study, and interpret fossil evidence from prehistoric times. By charting the kinds of fossils they discover and their positions in strata layers, paleontologists know much about the creatures that once lived in the Western Interior Seaway and along the regions that bordered it.

Marine Reptiles, Birds, and Fish Discovered Along the Western Interior Seaway

1. Grand Prairie, Alberta—Plesiosaur—2012
2. Mildred Lake, Alberta—Elasmosaur (plesiosaur)—2011
3. Carrot River, Saskatchewan—*Terminonaris* (crocodile)—1991
4. Wilson River, Manitoba—*Terminonaris* (crocodile)—2007
5. Thornhill, Manitoba—*Tylosaurus* (mosasaur)—1974 (a.k.a. "Bruce")
6. Morden, Manitoba—*Xiphactinus* (fish)—2010
7. Morden, Manitoba—*Enchodus* (fish)—2013
8. Morden, Manitoba—*Hesperornis* (bird)—2010
9. Cooperstown, North Dakota—*Archelon* (turtle)—2004
10. Lewis and Clark Lake, border of Nebraska and South Dakota—Mosasaur—2000
11. Smoky Hill River, Kansas—*Tusoteuthis* (squid)—2011
12. Smoky Hill Chalk, Kansas—*Clidastes* (mosasaur)—1995
13. Lewisville, Texas—*Terminonaris* (crocodile)—2006

Dinosaurs Outside Seaway (or in some cases bordering or overlapping the Seaway)

14. Mildred Lake, Alberta—Ankylosaur—2015
15. Dinosaur Provincial Park, near Brooks, Alberta—*Ornithomimus*—2009
16. Eastend, Saskatchewan—*Tyrannosaurus rex*—1991
17. Williston Lake, British Columbia—*Allosaurus* & *Ankylosaurus* tracks—2015
18. Spirit River, Alberta—Hadrosaur—2013
19. Newcastle, Wyoming—*Triceratops*—2013
20. Faith, South Dakota—*Tyrannosaurus rex*—1990
21. Dickinson County, Iowa—possible Hadrosaur—2000
22. Price, Utah—Stegosaur tracks—1996
23. Baker, Montana—*Tyrannosaurus rex*—2002
24. Delta, Colorado—*Supersaurus*—1972
25. Atoka County, Oklahoma—*Sauroposeidon proteless*—1994 (world's tallest dinosaur)

THE AGE OF REPTILES

Scientists estimate that the Earth is approximately 4.54 billion years old. That's a huge number. To appreciate its size, imagine a book with 4.54 billion pages. Each page represents one year. The first page tells about the present. The last page tells about the very beginnings of Earth's history.

With 4.54 billion pages, this is a thick book, almost 468,000 metres tall. That's like having fifty-two Mount Everests stacked one upon the other. To navigate through the book of time, scientists divide it into four chapters or eras:

Precambrian era—before abundant life appears;

Paleozoic era—ancient life (541 to 252 million years ago);

Mesozoic era—middle life (252 to 66 million years ago); and

Cenozoic era—recent life (66 million years ago to the present).

Modern humans have only been on Earth for approximately 200,000 years. That's less than 1% of our planet's age. But dinosaurs and marine reptiles lived here far earlier and for far longer during the Mesozoic era.

PRECAMBRIAN ERA
BEFORE ABUNDANT LIFE

PALEOZOIC ERA
ANCIENT LIFE FLOURISHES

541 MILLION YEARS AGO
LIFE FIRST APPEARS

The Mesozoic era is sometimes called the Age of Reptiles. It is divided into three periods. Dinosaurs and marine reptiles first appeared on Earth during the Triassic period (252 to 201 million years ago). Over time, they evolved. While some species died, new ones rose to take their place. By the Jurassic period (201 to 145 million years ago), their numbers had grown. During the Cretaceous period (145 to 66 million years ago), dinosaurs dominated the land while marine reptiles ruled the sea. Then, abruptly, everything changed. About sixty-six million years ago, a colossal wave of extinction took its toll and wiped out many species, dinosaurs and most marine reptiles included.

MESOZOIC ERA
AGE OF REPTILES

CENOZOIC ERA
AGE OF MAMMALS

TRIASSIC PERIOD

JURASSIC PERIOD

CRETACEOUS PERIOD

252 MILLION YEARS AGO
DINOSAURS AND MARINE REPTILES FIRST APPEAR

66 MILLION YEARS AGO
DINOSAURS AND MARINE REPTILES DISAPPEAR

200,000 YEARS AGO
MODERN HUMANS APPEAR

MARINE REPTILES

CHARACTERISTICS OF MARINE REPTILES

- Aquatic animals
- Flippers or fins stick out from sides
- Some are egg-layers, others are livebearers
- Carnivores

CLOSEST RELATIVE: modern-day crocodiles

SHARED CHARACTERISTICS

- Vertebrates, i.e., animals with backbones
- Air-breathers
- Possibly warm-blooded
- Lived during the Mesozoic era (252 to 66 million years ago)
- Now extinct, except for turtles

DINOSAURS

CHARACTERISTICS OF DINOSAURS

- Land-dwellers
- Four limbs
- Legs directly below hips
- Mostly egg-layers
- Some carnivores, others herbivores or omnivores

CLOSEST RELATIVE: modern-day birds

11

FORMATION OF THE WESTERN INTERIOR SEAWAY

About 300 million years ago, most of the land on Earth was joined into one huge landmass called Pangaea. This supercontinent covered nearly a third of the planet's surface and was surrounded by a giant ocean known as Panthalassa (*see The Earth's Interior*).

Around the end of the Triassic period, Pangaea started to break apart. Much like a jigsaw puzzle floating on a pool of molasses, Pangaea floated on top of the Earth's mantle. Convection currents in the mantle shifted the Earth's plates, moving them apart a few centimetres a year. As continents drifted free, landmasses slammed into others, pushing up folds of land along the coastal regions of North America, spiking up to form the Rocky Mountains, and spawning a torrent of volcanic activity.

Temperatures rose. The Earth's ice caps melted, causing a worldwide rise in sea levels. Because the middle of the North American continent was lower in elevation than surrounding ocean levels, water flooded the central regions, creating a large, shallow inland sea.

The Western Interior Seaway stretched from the Arctic Ocean to the Gulf of Mexico, a distance of 3200 kilometres (2000 miles). At its largest, it was 760 metres (2500 feet) deep and 970 kilometres (600 miles) wide.

The Earth's Interior

The inner Earth is composed of three main parts: the crust, the mantle, and the core.

Crust—an outer layer of rock that ranges in thickness, but averages from 30 to 50 kilometres (about 20 to 30 miles) thick and is made of seven major plates and nine minor ones. The crust is thickest under the continents and thinnest under the oceans.

Mantle—a layer 2900 kilometres (about 1800 miles) thick below the crust that is composed mostly of iron and magnesium.

Core—a sphere at the centre of the Earth that is made of two parts. The inner core is composed of solid iron about 1220 kilometres (760 miles) thick. A liquid outer core surrounds the inner core. Composed of a nickel-iron alloy, the outer core is about 2300 kilometres (1400 miles) thick.

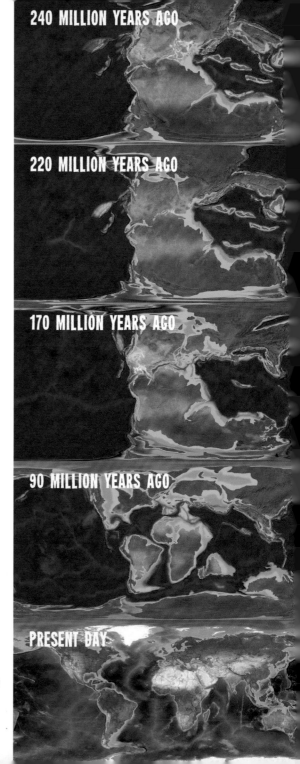

240 MILLION YEARS AGO

220 MILLION YEARS AGO

170 MILLION YEARS AGO

90 MILLION YEARS AGO

PRESENT DAY

CLIMATE AND CONDITIONS OF THE WESTERN INTERIOR SEAWAY

In the Cretaceous period, earthquakes, volcanic eruptions, dramatic climate changes, and shifts of the Earth's crust altered the North American landscape. Ash and other deposits—some from the older Appalachian Mountains in the east, more from the volatile Rocky Mountains in the west—filtered into the Western Interior Seaway, raising acidity levels and temperatures.

For much of the Cretaceous period, levels of carbon dioxide rose to one-and-a-half times their current levels. The Earth's average temperature was 20°C (68°F), about 6°C (11°F) higher than today. In these warm, steamy conditions, life flourished in the shallow sea. Algae multiplied. Plankton and tiny ammonites thrived, providing a blanket of food for other species. Predatory marine reptiles like the mighty mosasaur chased lesser creatures like fish, squid, and sea turtles. Flightless birds swam in the tepid sea and roamed the shoreline.

Over the lifetime of the Western Interior Seaway, boundaries shifted often, particularly along the highly active western shoreline. Sediment layered the bottom, rising and folding with shifting conditions. Locked in the strata, a permanent record of life in the Cretaceous period remains. Cemented into sandstone and shale formations, chalky bluffs, and bentonite layers are the fossils of creatures that once ruled the Western Interior Seaway.

GREAT MOMENTS IN GEOLOGY AND MARINE PALEONTOLOGY

DEPICTION OF AN EARLY MOSASAUR DISCOVERY

1780—Quarrymen working in a shaft 27 metres (90 feet) below the surface at Maastricht in the Netherlands unearth the skull and spinal column of a strange new creature. Because it is found along the Meuse River, this first-of-its-kind beast is given the name mosasaur (Latin *mosa* for the Meuse River, and *sauros* meaning lizard). Today, the fossil remains of the first mosasaur are on display at the Teylers Museum in Haarlem, Netherlands.

1811—While walking along the English coast after a storm had torn away part of a cliff, eleven-year-old Mary Anning spots a bone protruding from the dirt and discovers the first complete skeleton of an ichthyosaur, an ancient reptile that looks similar to a dolphin. Over her lifetime, Mary Anning discovers other fossil treasures including the first two plesiosaur skeletons ever found, and she goes down in history as one of the best fossil hunters ever.

1892—In his father's quarry in Holzmaden, Germany, Bernhard Hauff discovers the remains of an ichthyosaur complete with fragments of skin. It was the world's first glimpse of the outside covering of an extinct marine reptile. Since then, thousands of marine fossils have been discovered in quarries around Holzmaden, making it one of the richest deposits of fossils on the planet.

1912—German scientist Alfred Wegener reads a journal article that lists fossils discovered around the world. Curious about how some of the same fossils appear on more than one continent, even though oceans separate them, Wegener studies world maps. Like puzzle pieces, the bulge on the east coast of North America seems to fit into the contours of Europe. Similarly, the east coast of South America seems to fill a void on the west coast of Africa. To explain the phenomenon, Wegener proposes the continental drift theory.

A LETTER FROM MARY ANNING ABOUT ONE OF HER PLESIOSAUR DISCOVERIES

1918—In the chalky soil of Kansas, paleontologist Charles H. Sternberg discovers a *Tylosaurus* skeleton with the bones of a juvenile plesiosaur inside the rib cage, proof of the mosasaur's voracious appetite. Writes a surprised Sternberg, "this huge Tylosaur, that was about 29 feet long, had swallowed this plesiosaur in large enough chunks to include the stomach. How powerful the gastric juice that could dissolve these big bones!"

1938—On a visit to the docks of East London, South Africa, Marjorie Courtenay-Latimer, curator of a local museum, spots a blue fin poking out of a pile of fish. She digs out an odd-looking specimen—a heavily armoured fish, thickly scaled, with knobby fins that look more like legs. It's a coelacanth, a prehistoric fish thought to have been extinct for sixty-six million years. Courtenay-Latimer's discovery raises a question: Are there other plants and animals we assume are extinct, but are really very much alive?

MARJORIE COURTENAY-LATIMER POSING WITH HER COELACANTH DISCOVERY

1952—In the Smoky Hills region of Kansas, George F. Sternberg unearths a "fish-within-a-fish"—a 4 metre (13 feet) *Xiphactinus* with a 2 metre (6 feet) *Gillicus* inside its skeleton. Speculation has it that the larger fish swallowed the smaller one whole, then died after choking on its meal.

THE STERNBERG "FISH-WITHIN-A-FISH" SHOWS A 6-FOOT-LONG GILLICUS INSIDE THE LARGER XIPHACTINUS

1974—Ten kilometres west of Morden, Manitoba, a farmer investigates a fence post that has mysteriously turned up in his pasture. He discovers that the post is not a post after all, but the fossilized jawbone of a mosasaur. Excavations unearth a 13 metre (43 feet) *Tylosaurus*. Nicknamed "Bruce," and later displayed at the Canadian Fossil Discovery Centre, it enters the record books as the world's largest publicly exhibited mosasaur.

SKULL OF "BRUCE" THE MOSASAUR

1980—Walter Alvarez, an American geologist, notices high concentrations of iridium, a rare metal, in layers of rock just above those containing fossils from the Cretaceous period. Based on this discovery, Alvarez and his father, Luis, a physicist, propose that sixty-six million years ago an iridium-rich asteroid smashed into the Earth, spewing dust, blocking out the sun, and eventually killing many life forms, dinosaurs and marine reptiles included.

1990—Scientists find evidence supporting the Alvarez theory when they test rock samples from a giant crater almost 180 kilometres (about 110 miles) across that was first discovered in the Yucatán Peninsula in 1978. Seared into the sixty-six-million-year-old rock, they find materials formed under explosive, high-heat situations like those of an asteroid impacting the Earth.

FOSSILS HERE, FOSSILS THERE

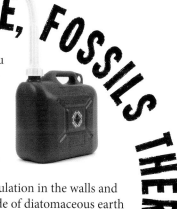

Even though you may not realize it, fossils surround you. Fill your car with gas, and you are using fossil fuels created millions of years ago from ancient plants and animals. Change the filter in your furnace, swish wax on your car, or stuff insulation in the walls and you might be using a product made of diatomaceous earth that contains microscopic, fossilized plankton. Sling a necklace bearing a nugget of amber around your neck, and you are proudly wearing a fossilized chunk of tree sap. **Fossils are here, there, everywhere.**

15

THE FOSSIL EVIDENCE

Picture a crime scene. A bank has been robbed overnight. Crumpled receipts from a convenience store litter the floor. Muddy footprints trail through the building. A wad of chewing gum lies near the door.

The clues are few, but to a crime scene investigator each shred of evidence tells a story. The crumpled receipts might tell police where the criminal shops and perhaps lives. Footprints indicate whether the thief worked alone, whether they were made by a man or woman, and perhaps even suggest the thief's height and weight. Chewing gum contains DNA that might reveal the thief's identity

CRIME SCENE DO NOT E

In much the same way, fossils provide clues to the past. Like the evidence collected at a crime scene, they tell a story, only their story is millions of years old. Instead of crime scene investigators, paleontologists and forensic experts gather and interpret the clues, looking to answer key questions. **What happened? Why? How? When?**

HOW MANY FOSSIL CLUES CAN YOU SPOT?

CRIME SCENE DO NOT ENTER

BECOMING A FOSSIL—NOT SO EASY

Take a bucket of food scraps and bury them in the ground. A few months later, dig them up. Chances are there won't be much left. Vegetables, fruits, breads, and other soft-tissue substances will likely have vanished. A few bones might remain, but little else.

The Earth is a very efficient decomposer, and that's a good thing for all of us. Imagine the mountains of waste that would accumulate otherwise. To keep the Earth's compost heap operating, decomposers convert the dead into useful material. Scavengers like vultures and crows feast on dead animals; insects like ants and termites digest waste; bacteria break down soft tissue and transform it into chemicals.

The Earth's agents of decomposition are a capable bunch—so effective that it's mighty unusual for anything dead to escape their attention. Soft body parts like skin, muscle tissue, and organs are the first to go. Bones, teeth, and claws take longer. Harder, sturdier parts like these have a better chance of surviving decomposition, making them the most likely to become fossils. Even so, the odds are against preservation unless conditions are just right.

To become a fossil, bodies need to be sheltered from decomposers. Those that are covered quickly with sediment have the best chances at fossilization. With its warm, shallow waters teeming with ash and other deposits, the Western Interior Seaway offered perfect conditions for quick burials. Odds for fossilization were better in the Seaway than along the land beside it.

TRUE FORM FOSSILS

Fossils that resemble the once-living organism or its parts but are composed of hardened minerals instead of tissue and bone are called true form fossils.

To become a true form fossil, bone has to turn to stone. Although organic parts of bones like blood cells, proteins, and fat eventually decompose, minerals like calcium and other inorganic components last longer. After organic parts disappear, minerals move in and retain the original shape. This happens when water seeps into microscopic pores and cavities, carrying minerals from the surrounding sediment, like iron, calcium carbonate, and silica. Over time and under pressure, the minerals stabilize and preserve the structure, turning it into a rock-like replica of the original.

OTHER WAYS TO DODGE DECOMPOSITION

Not everything preserved from the past takes on a rock-hard form. Nature has other ways to showcase the plants and creatures that once flourished in or around the Western Interior Seaway:

CARBONIZATION

When plant matter or animal tissue decay under water, gases like oxygen, hydrogen, and nitrogen are produced. Carbon molecules, which are more stable, remain as a thin black or brown carbon film.

FREEZING

Rapid freezing preserves a body's soft tissue. Finding still-frozen remains is rare and is usually restricted to animals like the ice age mammoth and rhinoceros. Both lived millions of years after dinosaurs and marine reptiles.

MUMMIFICATION

In dry, usually very warm, or extremely cold conditions, moisture escapes from dead tissue, leaving the remains dried and preserved.

AMBER PRESERVATION

Conifers like pine and spruce ooze sap or resin, sometimes trapping insects, pollen, spores, and other matter in the sticky fluid. With time, the resin hardens and is transformed into rock-hard amber, locking the perfectly preserved organism inside.

MORE FOSSIL TYPES

MOLDS—For some fossils, instead of the organism or its parts, an impression remains. Molds are formed when tissue or bone dissolves or rots away, leaving an imprint of the original in the surrounding rock.

CASTS—Casts are copies of the original. Casts form when tissue or bone dissolve, leaving a cavity in rock that later fills with minerals.

TRACE FOSSILS—Trace fossils are leftovers from prehistoric animals that tell about their activities or behaviour. Trace fossils include such things as footprints, eggs, dens, burrows, nests, stomach contents, and coprolite (dung).

CEDAR LAKE'S AMBER GOLD

The Saskatchewan River flows from Alberta to north-central Manitoba. Before entering Lake Winnipeg, it passes through Cedar Lake. At the mouth of Cedar Lake, where the swiftly moving Saskatchewan River converges with the lake's calmer waters, the river slows. Rocks, shells, and other deposits carried by the river sift to the bottom. Among the deposits lie chunks of amber from the Cretaceous period that have been carried from the valleys around Red Deer, Alberta.

For paleontologists, Cedar Lake's amber is like hidden treasure. Dozens of new species of insects and spiders have been discovered in the amber deposits, making Cedar Lake one of the world's most abundant and diverse sources of Cretaceous fossils.

CEDAR LAKE, MANITOBA

WHAT FOSSILS TELL US ABOUT PREHISTORIC LIFE

Each discovery, no matter how small, adds a new piece of information. Taken together, they tell us much about life long before humans appeared on planet Earth.

BONES: Fossilized bones tell us about a creature's structure, its size, how it looked, and its relationship to other living things.

TEETH: A jaw full of teeth says a lot about a creature, but even a single tooth can reveal important information about its diet and eating habits:

Broad, conical, sharp, recurved (pointing backwards) teeth
Perfect for: seizing, subduing, and slicing prey
Prehistoric example: mosasaur; *Modern-day example:* killer whale

Slender, pointed, conical teeth
Perfect for: seizing, piercing or gouging, and holding on to slippery prey
Prehistoric example: Xiphactinus; *Modern-day example:* dolphin

Long, slender, pointed teeth that interlock when jaw closes
Perfect for: trapping and "caging" smaller creatures before swallowing them whole
Prehistoric example: plesiosaur; *Modern-day example:* crabeater seal

SKIN: From skin impressions, scientists learn about a prehistoric animal's exterior covering. *Was it scaly or smooth? How thick was it?* On very rare occasions, skin pigment stains the rock, leaving a splash of colour that tells about the creature's behaviour. *Was its colour for camouflage, to signal to mates, or to flash a warning to potential enemies?*

TRACKS AND SWIM PATTERNS: Footprint tracks and swim patterns in rock say a lot about a creature's movement. *How did it propel itself? How fast did it move? Did it travel alone or in a group?* By measuring the size and depth of the tracks, scientists can estimate the animal's size and weight, too.

COPROLITE: Coprolite is fossilized dung. By studying coprolite, scientists learn about an animal's food sources and its digestive habits. *What did it eat? Where did it find food? How did it prey upon others?*

EGGS: *Were creatures of the Western Interior Seaway egg-layers? How many young did they have? How did they care for them?* These are the types of questions that fossil eggs can answer.

WHAT FOSSILS TELL US ABOUT OUR PLANET

It's evolutionary, my dear Mr. Watson—Fossils show that some prehistoric creatures bore a strong resemblance to those around us, suggesting that life evolved slowly from a few simple ancestors to the wide variety of organisms that now inhabit our planet.

Once a sea, not always a sea—Paleontologists have discovered seashells on the Himalayas, fossils of ichthyosaurs in the outbacks of Australia, and remains of sea turtles on the Canadian prairies, more proof that the Earth is a turbulent and constantly changing place.

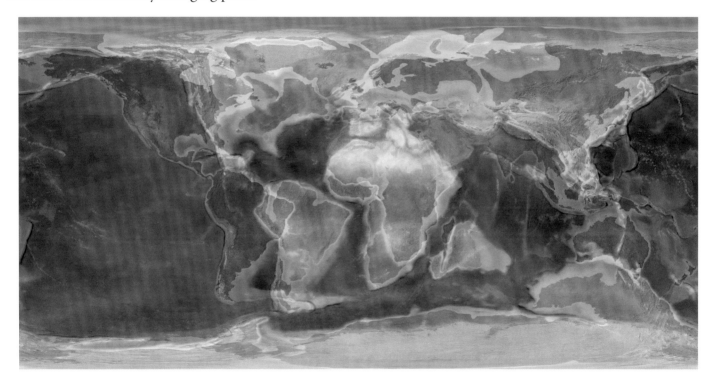

Help! We're adrift—Identical fossils found in similar beds of rock, oceans apart, provide evidence that the Earth's crust is composed of slowly moving plates. Don't expect any sudden changes, though. Even the most swiftly moving plates travel only 2 or 3 centimetres (1 inch) a year.

Climate change is real, man—Fossils of ferns found in Antarctica, magnolias in Greenland, and coral within the Arctic Circle show that at one time these were tropical areas. Fossils of muskoxen in Arkansas and reindeer in France suggest that these were frigid zones. Climate flip-flops have occurred in the past, and will likely happen in the future, though not necessarily for the same reasons.

SHALE

CHALK

BENTONITE

WHERE FOSSILS HIDE

To locate fossils, paleontologists often consult geologic maps. Geologic maps show the kinds and ages of rocks in different locations. Before looking for fossils, paleontologists scan geologic maps for locations where sedimentary rocks from the Cretaceous period are exposed at the Earth's surface.

Along the Western Interior Seaway, three types of sedimentary rock are common sources of fossils—**shale, chalk, and bentonite:**

Shale is a fine-grained soft rock, usually red, green, grey, or black in colour depending on the minerals that compose it. Shale forms when tiny particles of feldspar, quartz, mica, and pyrite erode off larger rocks, settle at the bottom of the ocean, sea, or lake, and mix with decaying organic material. Under pressure, layers cement together, sealing fossils inside.

A band of shale cuts a swath across the Western Interior Seaway. Known as the Pierre Shale, it can be found in Alberta, Saskatchewan, Manitoba, North Dakota, South Dakota, Montana, Colorado, Minnesota, New Mexico, Wyoming, Nebraska, and other places. In some settings, the Pierre Shale is 600 metres (about 2000 feet) thick; in others, as little as 200 metres (about 650 feet).

Chalk is a soft, white, porous sedimentary rock, composed of calcium carbonate. Chalk is formed when microscopic skeletons of plankton and other shelled creatures accumulate on the sea floor, forming a slurry of lime mud. Over time, heat and pressure compact the sediment, transforming it into chalk.

The Smoky Hills of western Kansas is one region along the Western Interior Seaway that contains outcroppings of chalk, making it a prime source of marine fossils from the Cretaceous period.

Bentonite is a type of clay formed when ash from volcanic eruptions settles in water, collecting minerals as it deposits in layers. Bentonite varies in colour from creamy white to yellow.

The region around Morden, Manitoba is blanketed with deposits of bentonite. Embedded between the layers of clay lie many fossils from the Cretaceous period.

GEOLOGIC MAP OF NORTH AMERICA

Geologic Time Scale
Millions of Years Ago

0	Quaternary
	Neogene
	Paleogene
65	Cretaceous
	Jurassic
	Triassic
240	Permian
	Pennsylvanian
	Mississippian
	Devonian
	Silurian
	Ordovician
	Cambrian
540	Late Proterozioc
	Middle Proterozioc
	Early Proterozioc
	Late Archean
	Middle Archean
4000	Early Archean
	Glacial Ice
	Age Unknown

25

BRUCE ... KING OF THE SEA?

Bruce, the world's largest publically exhibited mosasaur, is a *Tylosaurus* and the star attraction at the Canadian Fossil Discovery Centre in Morden, Manitoba. At 13 metres (43 feet), Bruce is the length of a city bus and bigger than a *T. rex*. Bruce's skull alone is almost as large as a refrigerator. With a double-hinged jaw and a massive bite, Bruce was capable of snagging prey equal in size to a horse. Once trapped on Bruce's two sets of recurved teeth, the game was over. Bruce finished off the meal by shredding it to pieces.

Bruce was discovered in 1974 within the Pembina Shale just north of Thornhill, Manitoba when a farmer investigated what looked like an out-of-place fence post in a pasture. The post turned out to be the jawbone of an immense mosasaur. It took two seasons to unearth, jacket, and move the skeleton which was 65–70% complete.

Excavators at the site named the colossal creature after a popular Monty Python skit in which every character bore the name Bruce. But in 2003, as a lightweight replica of Bruce was being prepared for display, workers at the Canadian Fossil Discovery Centre made a surprising discovery. Along the tail, Bruce had three equal-sized chevrons (triangle-shaped bones), which, according to one theory at the time, meant the world's largest mosasaur was a female, not a male as originally thought. This theory has since been discredited. There is currently no way to tell if Bruce is a male or female mosasaur.

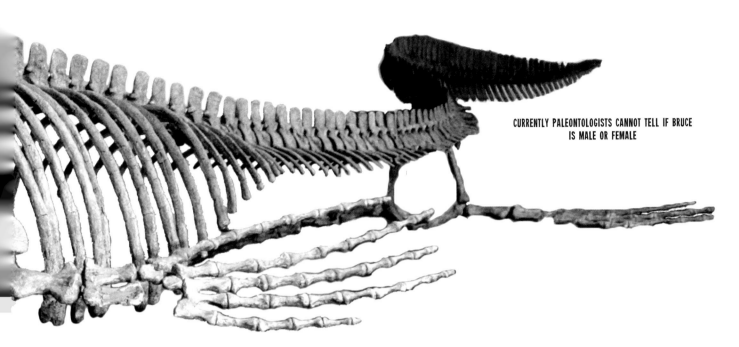

CURRENTLY PALEONTOLOGISTS CANNOT TELL IF BRUCE
IS MALE OR FEMALE

HOW BRUCE BECAME A FOSSIL ... AND WAS FOUND

- Eighty million years ago, Bruce died.

- Bruce's body sank to the bottom of the sea. Ash from Rocky Mountain volcanoes settled on the mud of the sea floor to form bentonite, a mineralized clay. Bentonite and other sediments quickly covered Bruce.

- The flesh rotted. Minerals like calcium carbonate infiltrated the microscopic pores of the bones and teeth, depositing their mineral content.

- Under pressure, the sediment became rock.

- The Western Interior Seaway drained, leaving fossilized Bruce sealed beneath land that was once the floor of the sea.

- Millions of years of erosion by wind, water, and ice churned the rock and wore down the surface.

- In 1974, a farmer discovered Bruce's fossilized and exposed jawbone. Excavations carried out over two years laid bare Bruce's impressive skeleton.

FROM FIELD TO LAB—BRINGING A FOSSIL HOME

Finding a fossil is one thing. Getting it out of the ground intact without losing valuable information is another. To safely bring fossils home, paleontologists follow an exacting process:

A) EXPOSE

With shovels and picks, paleontologists carefully dig around the perimeter of the fossil, then fan outward to determine its size and how far it extends. After removing the overburden (rock deposited on top), they use dental picks, brushes, and trowels to chip away the thinnest surface layers.

B) RECORD

Keeping records of a fossil's in situ (original) position is essential. Once the fossil is exposed, the site is photographed. A grid is constructed on the ground. Then a site map is drawn with coordinates that match the grid. Paleontologists mark the specimen on the map and assign it a number that matches its location in the grid.

C) TRENCH AND BLOCK

A trench is dug around the entire specimen. By undercutting it, paleontologists leave the bones on a pedestal smaller than the block above it. Very large fossils are undercut in several places to create smaller blocks for easier removal.

D) STABILIZE

Fossils that are fragile need to be stabilized before removal. Paleontologists apply a consolidant or hardening solution, if needed. It seeps into the fossil and hardens it from the inside out, making it more rigid and stable.

EXPOSE

RECORD

TRENCH AND BLOCK

WRAP AND TRANSPORT

REMOVE MATRIX AND JACKET

S. 74. 01. 02

CATALOGUE

E) WRAP IN A FIELD JACKET

A field jacket is an outer covering of plaster that is wrapped around the fossil and the rock left around it. It acts like a cast to protect the specimen for transport to the lab. First, paleontologists layer damp towels or paper around the specimen so it is easier to remove the plaster later. Next, they soak strips of burlap in plaster of Paris and, starting at the bottom of the block, drape them around the specimen. For extra strength, several layers are applied, then the jacket is allowed to dry and harden.

F) UNDERCUT AND TRANSPORT

To loosen the jacket containing the matrix (the fossil embedded in the block), paleontologists chisel around it, then flip it over to cover the underside and carefully transport it to the lab. This step is very delicate since there is a risk the fossil can fall out of the jacket.

G) REMOVE MATRIX AND JACKET

In the lab, paleontologists cut open the field jacket with a saw. Using dental picks and fine drills, they remove the matrix to expose the underside of the fossil. If necessary, more hardener is applied. To remove fine material, they use an air scribe to blow away dust. The fossil is photographed and closely inspected with magnifying glasses and microscopes.

H) CATALOGUE

A catalogue number is assigned to the fossil. This is a code that indicates what the fossil is, when it was found, and where it was found. An index card with all the information about the find is prepared, then filed for future reference. Data is charted on a computer for easy reference later.

RECONSTRUCTING THE PAST

Most excavations yield partial skeletons, rarely an entire specimen. Often, bones are missing. Some may have been carried off by predators or scavengers. Others may have decomposed before or during fossilization. Still others might have been swept away during floods, or became buried in other locations after separating from the body. With only partial skeletons to work with, how do we know what extinct creatures looked like or how they moved?

Fortunately, paleontologists are skilled at extracting clues. Strange as it might seem, many of the clues lie in the present rather than in the long-dead past. Here are some of the things scientists and paleoartists do to understand and reconstruct extinct creatures:

FILL IN THE GAPS—Even if our specimen is missing bones, chances are that it's not the only one in existence. By combining information from different partial skeletons, scientists can better understand how the complete skeleton might have looked. Museums often share knowledge and specimens. If a museum needs information, such as photos or replicas of missing limbs, they can consult other museums with similar collections.

STUDY ITS RELATIVES—Fortunately, individuals of the same family tend to look and act in similar ways. Suppose scientists discover a few bones from a new genus of mosasaur. Although they may not know exactly how it looked, they can learn a lot about the size, shape, and number of missing bones by comparing the new mosasaur to others in its family.

STUDY THE LIVING—Animals with similar bone structures and joints hold their bodies in similar ways. By studying the posture and movement of living animals, scientists can determine how extinct creatures with similar structures might have looked and moved.

BUILDING "BRUCE" THE MOSASAUR

CHECK THOSE MUSCLES—Muscles and tendons attached to hips, shoulders, and skulls often leave tiny scars on fossilized bone. By studying attachment scars and comparing them to similar features on the bones of living animals, scientists can figure out the size, shape, and location of muscles on the extinct creature. For example, if attachment scars bear a strong resemblance to those of an elephant, scientists and paleoartists know that they need to "beef-up" the muscles on the extinct animal.

SCAN THE SKULL—With modern-day CT scans, we can learn a lot about how dinosaurs and marine reptiles functioned. For example, in 2003, CT scans of pterosaur skulls showed that the flying reptile likely had a specialized brain and inner ear structure that allowed it to fly and target its prey. In 2008, other CT scans showed that dinosaurs have large airways inside their skulls. Scientists believe these airways reduced the weight of dinosaurs' heads, allowing them to make quick movements.

ADD CLOTHES—Was the animal covered in feathers, skin, or heavy armour? What colour was it? To replicate the outer covering on an extinct animal, scientists and paleoartists rely on the fossil evidence. Sometimes, if an animal is buried in fine sediment that hardens quickly before decomposition, the sediment retains skin impressions that indicate if the outer covering was smooth, scaly, knobby, or heavily plated. On rare occasions, skin pigments adhere to the rock, giving clues to the animal's true colour.

CREATE A COMPUTER MODEL—By using specialized software to input raw data such as the length and placement of bones, the thickness and location of muscles, and other features, it's sometimes possible to create a computer-generated model of an extinct creature. Rendered as a 3D image, the model can simulate the creature's looks and movements, and bring the past to life.

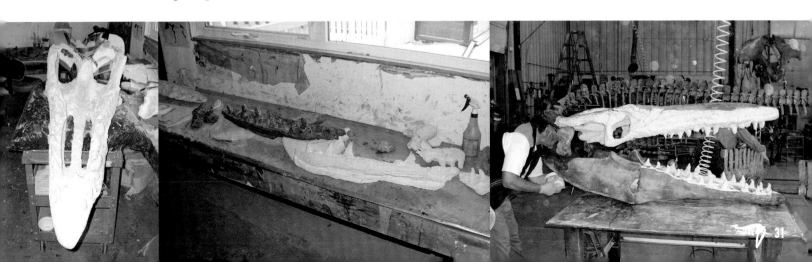

EVEN A LITTLE BONE CAN BE SPECIAL

Walk through a museum like the Canadian Fossil Discovery Centre and you'll see exhibits, photographs, and even entire replicas of mighty creatures that once swam the Western Interior Seaway or roamed the Earth. Thanks to hardworking curators, artists, and museum specialists, visitors are treated to carefully organized displays. Everything looks tidy, precise, and complete.

THIS *TRINACROMERUM* HANGS FROM THE CEILING OF THE CANADIAN FOSSIL DISCOVERY CENTRE

In contrast, paleontology is far less certain and a lot more fluid. Even a single bone can make a difference. With each new discovery, our bank of knowledge grows. What we understand about the past one day might be different the next.

Rarely does an entire specimen turn up intact. When the skull of a *Clidastes*, a type of mosasaur, was unearthed near Morden in 1974 with all parts present, it was an exciting moment. More often, bones are scattered, crushed, or broken. Even thick skulls might lie in pieces, and when fragments are missing, it takes a skilled analyst to reconstruct the puzzle and interpret the evidence.

Identifying a creature from just a few bones can be tricky, even when dealing with a species that is already well documented. The task becomes even more complicated if the bones are from a new species never seen before.

NEARLY COMPLETE SKULL OF A *CLIDASTES* MOSASAUR

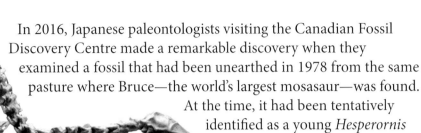

In 2016, Japanese paleontologists visiting the Canadian Fossil Discovery Centre made a remarkable discovery when they examined a fossil that had been unearthed in 1978 from the same pasture where Bruce—the world's largest mosasaur—was found. At the time, it had been tentatively identified as a young *Hesperornis regalis*—a flightless diving bird from the Cretaceous period. The specimen had been jacketed, moved into storage, and placed on a shelf until it could be studied closely.

RECREATED *HESPERORNIS* SKELETON IN A DIVING POSE AT THE CANADIAN FOSSIL DISCOVERY CENTRE

Four decades later, when visiting scientists picked through the fossilized remains and compared the bones with others of the same species, they noticed differences. The bones were not a perfect match to other *Hesperornis regalis*. Furthermore, the bird's leg bone lacked the growth marks typical of a juvenile bird. The scientists had found a hidden treasure—the first of an entirely new species of *Hesperornis*, and not a juvenile as first thought, but an adult.

REPLICA OF A *TERMINONARIS*'S HIND LIMB ON DISPLAY AT THE CANADIAN FOSSIL DISCOVERY CENTRE

Rather than name the new species after themselves, the paleontologists called it *Hesperornis lumgairi* to honour David Lumgair, the farmer who owns the property near Thornhill, Manitoba where a great many prehistoric creatures have been pulled from the ground.

FOSSIL REMAINS FROM A *HESPERORNIS LUMGAIRI*

BEHIND THE SCENES AT A FOSSIL MUSEUM

Beyond the carefully crafted exhibits that populate fossil museums, there are other spaces that look, sound, and even smell different. These are the laboratories and research areas where paleontologists, technicians, and volunteers unravel secrets sealed in rocks deposited eons ago.

Stepping into a fossil laboratory like the one at the Canadian Fossil Discovery Centre is an adventure all its own. Shelves wrap the walls. Cupboards fitted with drawers line the floor. Each shelf and drawer holds specimens found around the bentonite layers near Morden. Some specimens are tiny and delicate: fish scales, small teeth, hollow bird bones. Others are large and heavy: vertebrae, ribs, mandibles. Still more are encased in plaster jackets decades old. Labels roughly identify the contents, but what's inside doesn't always match the label. Opening the jacket is a bit like opening a box of assorted chocolates. Sometimes there are surprises inside.

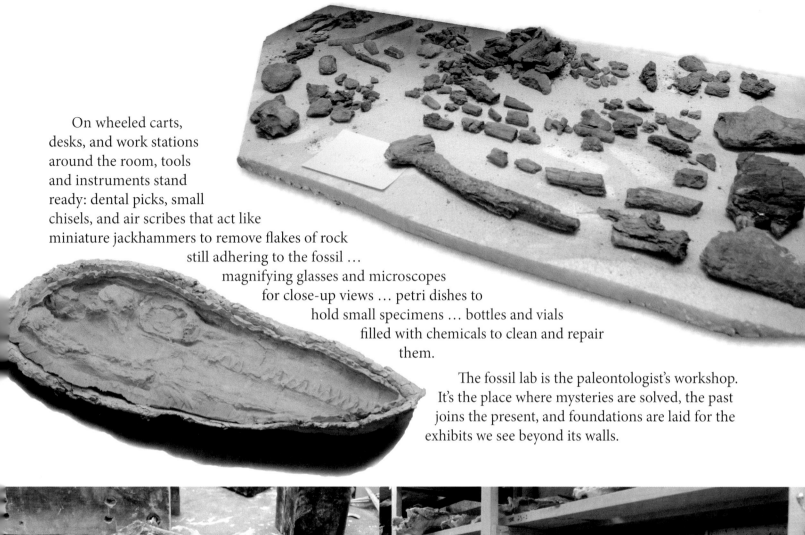

On wheeled carts, desks, and work stations around the room, tools and instruments stand ready: dental picks, small chisels, and air scribes that act like miniature jackhammers to remove flakes of rock still adhering to the fossil … magnifying glasses and microscopes for close-up views … petri dishes to hold small specimens … bottles and vials filled with chemicals to clean and repair them.

The fossil lab is the paleontologist's workshop. It's the place where mysteries are solved, the past joins the present, and foundations are laid for the exhibits we see beyond its walls.

ESTABLISHING A TIMELINE

TO DETERMINE A FOSSIL'S AGE, SCIENTISTS USE TWO METHODS:

RELATIVE DATING

Imagine a giant wastebasket filled with paper litter. Unless someone shook or stirred the contents, it's safe to say that the papers closer to the bottom were probably tossed into the bin before papers closer to the top. Layers at the bottom are older than ones above them. There's also a strong likelihood that items in the same layer might have been deposited around the same time.

Scientists use a similar method to determine the relative age of a fossil. Sedimentary rock forms when sediment piles up in layers and hardens into rock. Normally, the lower or deeper a layer, the older the sedimentary deposit. By establishing a fossil's position within the layers, and by comparing its position to layers above or below it, scientists can approximate a fossil's age.

Another way to estimate age is to compare fossils that lie in the same strata. If the age of one fossil is known, chances are that others in the strata are similar in age.

ABSOLUTE DATING

Scientists use radiometric dating to determine a fossil's exact age. Elements like potassium-40, uranium-238, and uranium-235, which are found in clay, mica, bentonite, and other mineral deposits, are radioactive. They decay or shed nuclear particles at a predictable rate and act like ticking clocks.

On nuclear clocks like these, the amount of time it takes for half of the atoms to decay is called a half-life. By figuring out the ratio of unchanged radioactive atoms to those that have shed particles, scientists can calculate a fossil's age.

Here's an example. The half-life of potassium-40 is close to 1.25 billion years. When potassium-40 sheds neutrons, it transforms into argon, an inert gas. Using a device called a mass spectrometer, scientists can measure the amount of potassium-40 in a sample. By comparing it to the amount of argon present, they determine where along the half-life scale the sample lies, and thus figure out its age.

NEWEST LAYERS

OLDEST LAYERS

INTERPRETING THE EVIDENCE

WITH EACH NEW FOSSIL DISCOVERY, QUESTIONS ABOUND. WHAT IS THIS? HOW DID THIS HAPPEN? WHEN? WHY? CAN YOU INTERPRET THE EVIDENCE TO FIGURE OUT WHAT LIKELY HAPPENED IN EACH OF THESE PUZZLING CASES?

Case #1

Paleontologists at the Canadian Fossil Discovery Centre discovered a strange triangle-shaped indentation in the tough connective tissue (pen) of a large squid unearthed near Morden, Manitoba. The indentation was the same shape and size as a mosasaur tooth. What happened?

Possible explanation:

Because the indentation is still visible, tissue had not yet grown over it, which indicates that the bite mark was fresh. Paleontologists believe the squid died in a battle with a hungry mosasaur.

Case #2

In 2014, fossils of several plesiosaurs were found on Melville Island in northern Canada. Because of the shape and size of the bones, scientists estimated that the plesiosaurs were mostly juveniles, perhaps a year or two old. What happened to the adult plesiosaurs? Where did they go?

Possible explanation:

The evidence suggests that juvenile plesiosaurs may have occupied different regions than adults. Young plesiosaurs may have inhabited shallower waters, closer to shore, perhaps for protection from predators. Faster, larger adults on the hunt for prey might have moved to the open seas.

Case #3

Over the past century, fossils of eight dinosaurs have been discovered in the Smoky Hills region of Kansas, near the middle of the once-mighty Western Interior Seaway. How did the remains of these land-dwellers end up hundreds of kilometres away from the Seaway's nearest coastline?

Possible explanation:

While floods or rising tides might have swept the dinosaurs out to sea, perhaps drowning them, another scenario is more likely. After dying near shore, the bodies decomposed in the warm water, accumulating enough gas in their abdomens to float the carcasses. Winds and currents carried the bloated bodies far away where they were scavenged by sharks or where their remains simply rotted apart and dropped to the sea floor.

Case #4

In 2008, miners near Lethbridge, Alberta uncovered the bones of a small mosasaur. When paleontologists examined it, they found fish bones inside the creature's gut and beneath its skeleton from a 1-metre-long (3 feet) fish called a "grinner." Bite marks along the fish bones matched the shape, size, and spacing of the mosasaur's teeth. But there were bite marks on the mosasaur's bones, too, and mixed with the other fossils, two sets of shark teeth. What happened?

Possible explanation:

Paleontologists suspect that the grinner was the mosasaur's last meal. Because fish bones were scattered inside and outside of the mosasaur, they figure the mosasaur nabbed the fish, chomped it into smaller pieces, and swallowed one chunk after the other. Shortly after, the mosasaur died, perhaps in an attack by another predator. At least three sharks scavenged the body. Two lost teeth; a third left bite marks.

LIFE IN THE WESTERN INTERIOR SEAWAY

For much of its existence, the Western Interior Seaway was a tropical place, swarming with a diversity of life. For predators, the Seaway was a thriving buffet of delights. In such prime conditions, many creatures in the Seaway not only survived, but also flourished. Some grew to colossal proportions, outstripping many land animals in size and ferocity. This is perhaps why so many of the world's greatest marine fossil discoveries have been made in what was once the Western Interior Seaway.

FISH (*XIPHACTINUS*)—LANE COUNTY, KS
5.6 METRES (18.5 FEET) LONG
WORLD'S LARGEST COMPLETE *XIPHACTINUS*

CROCODILE (*TERMINONARIS*)—LAKE LEWISVILLE, TX
96 MILLION YEARS AGO
WORLD'S OLDEST *TERMINONARIS* FOSSIL

MOSASAUR (*TYLOSAURUS*)—MORDEN, MB
13 METRES (43 FEET) LONG
WORLD'S LARGEST MOSASAUR ON PUBLIC DISPLAY

ICHTHYOSAUR (*SHONISAURUS*)—PINK MOUNTAIN, BC
23 METRES (75 FEET) LONG
WORLD'S LARGEST ICTHYOSAUR

TURTLE (*ARCHELON*)—BUFFALO GAP, SD
4 METRES (13 FEET) LONG, AND ABOUT 4.9 METRES
(16 FEET) WIDE FROM FLIPPER TO FLIPPER
WORLD'S LARGEST *ARCHELON*

SHARK (*CRETOXYRHINA*)—HACKBERRY CREEK, KS
5.3 METRES (17 FEET) LONG
LARGEST SHARK FOUND ALONG THE
WESTERN INTERIOR SEAWAY

PLESIOSAUR (ELASMOSAUR)—
BEARPAW FORMATION, AB
11.2 METRES (37 FEET) LONG
WORLD'S LONGEST PLESIOSAUR

MOSASAURS

Sometimes nicknamed the "T. Rex of the Sea" for their ferocious appetites and killer instincts, mosasaurs were the Western Interior Seaway's top predator during the Late Cretaceous period. Long and sleek, with paddle-like flippers and powerful, flattened tails, mosasaurs undulated through the water much like the snakes of today, swishing their tails to push themselves ahead. Mosasaurs accelerated from standing still to full speed in seconds, and changed directions quickly and easily. Camouflaged by dark, mottled skin and equipped with large lungs, mosasaurs could dive deep for long periods before resurfacing for air. With two sets of conical teeth, a flexible skull, and a moveable lower jaw that allowed for extra-wide bites, larger mosasaurs dined on whatever they pleased, from tiny ammonites to giant fish like *Xiphactinus*.

CLIDASTES (KLEE-DAS-TEEZ)
NAME MEANS: locked vertebrae

SIZE: up to 4 metres (13 feet) long   **DIET**: mostly fish

RANGE: shallows and coastal regions of the Western Interior Seaway

One of the smallest mosasaurs in the Western Interior Seaway, *Clidastes* was a skilled hunter. A short neck composed of interlocking vertebrae boosted its strength. Streamlined, agile, compact, and powered by whips of its thick muscular tail, *Clidastes* zipped along shallow waters near the coastline. Equipped with a double-hinged jaw set in an oversized head, *Clidastes* feasted largely on fish by piercing and locking on to its prey with sharp, recurved teeth.

PLATECARPUS (PLAT-E-CAR-PUS)

NAME MEANS: flat wrist **SIZE**: up to 7 metres (23 feet) long **DIET**: small fish, squid, mollusks, ammonites
RANGE: open waters of the Western Interior Seaway

Platecarpus was the most plentiful of the mosasaurs in the Western Interior Seaway. A tail reinforced on its upper side with rigid layers of large scales added strength, power, and speed to its movements. Nostrils positioned forward and on the side of a short snout likely meant that *Platecarpus* could detect scents, tell where they came from, what creature produced them, and even how far away its prey was. With a short snout, there was less room for teeth, forcing *Platecarpus* to hunt for smaller game or more bitable food such as fish, squid, and soft-shelled mollusks.

PLIOPLATECARPUS (PLY-OH-PLAT-E-KAR-PUS)

NAME MEANS: more flat wrist

SIZE: up to 6 metres (20 feet) long

DIET: fish, squid, ammonites

RANGE: shallower waters of the Western Interior Seaway

Free-roaming *Plioplatecarpus* frequented shallower waters. A snout studded with thick, recurved teeth meant that *Plioplatecarpus* probably snared and gripped its slippery prey, then chomped along its meal's body with rapid-fire bites. Eyes that were large compared to its short skull may have been a bonus, allowing *Plioplatecarpus* to see in low light conditions like those in deeper waters.

MORE MOSASAURS ...

HAINOSAURUS (HIGH-NOE-SORE-US)

NAME MEANS: Haino lizard (Haino refers to the valley of the Haine, Belgium where the first *Hainosaurus* was discovered)

SIZE: up to 13 metres (43 feet) long **DIET**: fish, sharks, plesiosaurs, turtles, squid, and smaller mosasaurs

RANGE: deeper waters of the Western Interior Seaway

One of largest mosasaurs in the Western Interior Seaway, *Hainosaurus* was also one of the strongest and most muscular. Swishes of its long, thick tail not only propelled *Hainosaurus* through the water, but may have helped fend off attacks from predators. Fine serrations along its teeth suggest that *Hainosaurus* hunted easily digested food like small-boned fish. Proof of its impressive appetite was found in Belgium where, embedded in the stomach contents of a *Hainosaurus*, paleontologists discovered the remains of a large turtle.

TYLOSAURUS (TIE-LO-SORE-US)

NAME MEANS: knob lizard

SIZE: up to 15 metres (49 feet) long

DIET: fish, sharks, flightless birds, plesiosaurs, other mosasaurs, and possibly carrion like dinosaurs

RANGE: deeper waters of the Western Interior Seaway

Tylosaurus was the deadliest and largest mosasaur in the Western Interior Seaway. *Tylosaurus* likely approached unsuspecting targets from below. Viewed from the front, with most of its huge length hidden behind, *Tylosaurus* probably looked less threatening to its prey than it actually was. Two special features made *Tylosaurus* an almost-invincible foe. Double rows of cone-shaped teeth set inside a powerful, wide jaw meant that few prey escaped its massive bite. *Tylosaurus* also had a blunt, reinforced snout that it might have used like a battering ram at high speeds.

Note: The most current research indicates that *Hainosaurus* and *Tylosaurus* may be the same species.

ICHTHYOSAURS

With their long snouts and sleek bodies, ichthyosaurs (ik-thee-uh-sawrs) looked similar to modern day porpoises and dolphins. Strong and fast swimmers, they pushed through the water by swishing their forked tails side-to-side. Four crescent-shaped fins and a dorsal fin provided stability. Mostly surface-dwellers, ichthyosaurs relied on a mixed diet of fish, octopus, and other swimming creatures.

Unlike fish, ichthyosaurs were not equipped with gills. Instead, they breathed air into their lungs through nostrils that were set close to oversized eyes near the top of their snouts. Extra-large eyes may have given ichthyosaurs the edge in deeper waters, allowing them to see their prey even in cloudy, darkened conditions.

Ichthyosaurs first appeared 250 million years ago during the Triassic period. During the Cretaceous period, their numbers dwindled. Scientists do not know exactly what caused their extinction, but the last ichthyosaurs disappeared ninety million years ago, long before a catastrophic event wiped out dinosaurs and marine reptiles.

Although many different kinds of ichthyosaurs occupied the Earth's seas and oceans, fossils of one variety— *Platypterygius* (flat wing)—have been found along the Western Interior Seaway. Up to 7 metres (23 feet) long and weighing between 1 and 2 tons, *Platypterygius* gave birth to its young in the water. Inside the stomach of one specimen, paleontologists discovered remnants of baby turtles and birds, which suggests that by the Late Cretaceous period *Platypterygius* might have broadened its diet in order to survive.

PLESIOSAURS

Picture a crocodile. Now picture a dolphin. Next imagine a new creature created from parts of both. Shrink the head, lengthen the neck, make the tail pointy, and give it four long flippers, two in the front and two at the back. Fill its mouth with sharp, spiked teeth. Now make it ten or twenty times larger and you might have something that resembles a plesiosaur.

Plesiosaurs had broad, barrel-shaped bodies that were flat along the bottom. A short tail served as a rudder and helped steer the plesiosaur as its long flippers propelled it through the water. With mouths filled with spiked teeth and, in some species, a jaw-bite strong enough to puncture sheet metal, plesiosaurs snared fish, squid, and mollusks before swallowing them whole.

Plesiosaurs populated the Western Interior Seaway throughout much of the Mesozoic era. By the Late Cretaceous period, their numbers had dwindled, possibly due to the arrival of new predators like mosasaurs. More plesiosaur fossils have been found in the northern regions of the Seaway, indicating that they may have preferred cooler waters or that factors like currents, oxygen levels, and changing salt concentrations could have driven them north.

ELASMOSAURUS (EL-LAZZ-MO-SORE-US)

NAME MEANS: thin plate lizard

SIZE: up to 14 metres (46 feet) long **DIET**: fish, squid, mollusks, and possibly clams and snails scooped from the bottom

RANGE: deeper, open waters of the Western Interior Seaway

Weighing as much as a mid-size car and as long as two minivans, *Elasmosaurus* was a deep-water hunter. A long, rigid neck consisting of seventy-one vertebrae—more than any living creature today—brought advantages and disadvantages. On the plus side, it gave *Elasmosaurus* sneak-attack capabilities. Approaching from below, with its small head perched away from its bulky body, the majority of its mass remained unseen. *Elasmosaurus* probably looked more like another fish or a water snake, rather than the predator it was. By reaching into schools of fish swimming above, *Elasmosaurus* surprised its prey and impaled its next meal on needle-point teeth before gulping it down. But its long neck probably brought difficulties, too. Because of its length and rigidity, *Elasmosaurus* lacked the flexibility to turn its neck sideways or the muscle strength to raise its head high above water.

DOLICHORHYNCHOPS (DOL-LEE-KOR-RIN-CHOPS)

NAME MEANS: long-nosed eye

SIZE: up to 5.5 metres (18 feet) long   **DIET**: fish

RANGE: shallow waters of the Western Interior Seaway

A short-necked plesiosaur with long, paddle-like fins, *Dolichorhynchops* flew through the water like an oversized penguin. Large eyes adapted for seeing small prey, smooth skin for speedy movements and deep dives, and long, narrow jaws filled with thirty to forty needle-like teeth in a single row made *Dolichorhynchops* a fearsome threat to fish along the Western Interior Seaway. Although well-equipped to grab and pierce its prey, *Dolichorhynchops* could not chew with its pinpoint teeth, but instead swallowed its captured fish whole.

TRINACROMERUM (TRY-NAH-KRO-ME-RUM)

NAME MEANS: three-tipped femur

SIZE: up to 3.3 metres (11 feet) long   **DIET**: fish

RANGE: mostly shallow waters of the Western Interior Seaway

Compared to *Elasmosaurus*, *Trinacromerum* had a much shorter neck and was much closer to *Dolichorhynchops* in habits and appearance. Sleek and strong, with elongated jaws filled with thin, piercing teeth, *Trinacromerum* sped through the water with ease, shifting directions to snag tasty fish or escape predators like sharks, mosasaurs, and larger plesiosaurs.

PLESIOSAUR BITS AND BITES

STONES AMONG BONES

Some plesiosaurs have been found with small stones, or gastroliths, in their stomachs. Because plesiosaurs lacked flattened teeth for chewing and likely swallowed their food whole, gulping down stones like these may have helped them to grind food during digestion. Another possibility: gastroliths may have been used as ballast or extra weight to help when diving.

TWO FOR ONE

While hiking in western Kansas in 1987, amateur paleontologist Chuck Bonner noticed the flat pelvic bones of a plesiosaur protruding out of the shale. Digging further, he located four flippers, ribs, hips, a spinal column, and part of the plesiosaur's neck.

In 2008, when paleontologists at the Natural History Museum in Los Angeles examined the specimen closely, they discovered miniature plesiosaur bones inside the larger fossil's abdomen. The evidence suggests that the larger plesiosaur was a pregnant female with a fetus growing inside. The discovery prompted scientists to re-evaluate their understanding of plesiosaurs. Rather than being egg-layers as originally thought, plesiosaurs are now thought to be livebearers who gave birth to their young in the water.

NESSIE—REAL OR NOT?

For centuries, people around Scotland's Loch Ness have claimed that a sea monster lurks in the lake's deep, cold waters. According to purported sightings, the creature looks a lot like an *Elasmosaurus*. "Nessie's" small head is perched on an extended neck. As it cuts through the water, Nessie's long body loops behind, barely rippling the surface.

Rumours abound. Some say Nessie once killed a man. Others maintain that they've spotted the creature lumbering across a nearby road before disappearing into the lake. Despite the claims, Nessie's existence seems to be more myth than reality. Grainy photographs of a shadowy form proved to be hoaxes, sonar failed to capture clear images, and submersibles trolling the lake didn't spot a single plesiosaur-like creature in the dark water.

A CASE OF MISTAKEN IDENTITY?

In 1977, Japanese fishermen off the coast of New Zealand found a very rotten carcass of a large creature with flippers. It was decomposed and difficult to identify. Some people believe that it was a plesiosaur. Scientists, however, are certain that it was a basking shark so decomposed that it had rotted to bits.

THE BONE WARS

In 1868, American paleontologist Edward Drinker Cope received a box of bones from a Kansas military doctor. After quick examination, Cope realized that the bones came from a new, odd-looking reptile—a plesiosaur. Naming the creature *Elasmosaurus*, Cope reconstructed the skeleton. Mistakenly, he attached the small head to the end of its short tail instead of its long neck. Another American paleontologist, Othniel C. Marsh, pointed out the error, embarrassing Cope and fueling a bitter rivalry known as the "Bone Wars."

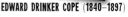

EDWARD DRINKER COPE (1840–1897)

Over the next two decades, the two tried to outdo each other. They sent agents to uncharted fossil beds in a race to be the first to locate new specimens. Both resorted to unsavory tactics: spying on each other's excavations, bribing employees, even stealing bones outright.

By the time Cope died in 1897, both he and Marsh had amassed an impressive but questionable record. Marsh had identified eighty new genera and species; Cope, fifty-six. Even in death, the rivalry continued. Certain that he was the more clever of the two, Cope made an unusual last request. He ordered that after death his head be severed and dissected so that his brain might be measured and compared to Marsh's. Marsh, who died two years later, declined the challenge. To this day, Cope's head remains in storage at the University of Pennsylvania.

OTHNIEL CHARLES MARSH (1831–1899)

FISH

Complete fossils of fish are rarely found. Teeth, scales, tiny bones, and vertebrae are quite common though, and they tell us much about the fish that once swam the Western Interior Seaway.

During the Late Cretaceous period, fish had many of the same features as fish today—a skeleton composed largely of bone, a body covered with protective scales, fins, tails, gills, and often a swim bladder that helped them to float or dive as needed. Most were carnivorous and preyed on smaller fish. But compared to modern fish, many were enormous. *Xiphactinus*, the largest fish in the Western Interior Seaway, was longer than the average great white shark while *Ichthyodectes*, at 4 metres (13 feet) long, ran a close second.

ENCHODUS (EN-COE-DUS)

NAME MEANS: spear tooth
SIZE: up to 1.5 metres (5 feet) long **DIET**: smaller fish
RANGE: throughout the Western Interior Seaway

Often called the "sabre-toothed herring" because of its large fangs, many species of *Enchodus* populated the Western Interior Seaway, ranging from very small varieties to some the length of a person. Judging by its downward sloping jaw, *Enchodus* likely approached its prey from underneath and behind, then caged its meal by trapping prey inside its mouth.

ICHTHYODECTES (IK-FEE-O-DEK-TEES)

NAME MEANS: fish biter with comb teeth

SIZE: up to 4 metres (13 feet) long **DIET**: other fish

RANGE: throughout the Western Interior Seaway

Long and sleek, *Ichthyodectes* looked much like a modern barracuda. It was covered with oval-shaped scales. Streamlined and muscular, it cruised at high speeds, effectively outmaneuvering its prey. Although capable of dodging many predators, *Ichthyodectes* was sometimes a meal for larger sea creatures such as its cousin *Xiphactinus*.

XIPHACTINUS (ZIF-ACK-TIH-NUS)

NAME MEANS: sword ray

SIZE: up to 6 metres (20 feet) long **DIET**: fish, seabirds

RANGE: surface-dweller along the Western Interior Seaway

With its bulldog-like expression, *Xiphactinus* looked menacing. An enormous body, blunted head, and rows of spiked teeth in a broad upturned jaw contributed to its ominous look. With one chomp of its huge, gaping mouth, *Xiphactinus* could swallow entire creatures up to 2 metres (6.5 feet) long. Those too large for a single bite were snared on its sharp teeth, unable to escape, allowing *Xiphactinus* to finish them off one mighty chomp at a time. It had a muscular body and a backbone of over 100 vertebrae. Powered by a strong forked tail and winged pectoral fins, *Xiphactinus* was one of the fastest and fiercest creatures in the Western Interior Seaway. Despite its size, *Xiphactinus* was not immune to attacks by other predators. *Xiphactinus* have been found in the fossilized stomach contents of a shark, suggesting that it was prey for others, too.

TURTLES

Turtles occupying the Western Interior Seaway during the Late Cretaceous period resembled turtles of today. Most had oval shaped bodies, protruding tails, and heads that extended forward. They breathed through lungs, propelled themselves with sweeps of their broad, powerful flippers, laid eggs on land, and survived on a mixed diet of fish and plants. Because modern turtles so closely resemble their Late Cretaceous relatives, they are sometimes called "living fossils."

Despite the similarities, there were differences, too, mostly in size. *Archelon*, for example, was a maxed out turtle, the size of a raft, and heavier than any turtle today. On the other end of the size scale, *Toxochelys* was much smaller and a more attractive mouthful for many predators than its larger cousin.

ARCHELON (ARK-KELL-ON)

NAME MEANS: ruling turtle

SIZE: up to 4 metres (13 feet) long and 4.9 metres (16 feet) wide, flipper to flipper

DIET: fish, jelly fish, squid, shell-fish, ammonites, plants

RANGE: Open waters, mostly southern parts of the Western Interior Seaway

Some paleontologists think that *Archelon* could have lived up to 100 years. Weighing as much as a rhinoceros, it was the largest turtle in the Western Interior Seaway. With its sharp, hooked beak, *Archelon* could crack open clams and other hard-shelled creatures. Four wide flippers powered *Archelon* through the water. To steer, it alternated movements of the front pair. Instead of a solid shell like many modern-day turtles, *Archelon* had a leathery covering supported by a skeletal framework and probably could not withdraw its head for protection. Despite its size, *Archelon* was defenceless in open water and a likely target for giant mosasaurs and sharks.

Although *Archelon* fossils have been found as far north as Canada, most are from the South Dakota, and Wyoming areas, suggesting that Archelon preferred warmer waters.

PROTOSTEGA (PRO-TOE-STEG-AH)

NAME MEANS: first roof

SIZE: up to 3 metres (10 feet) long

DIET: jellyfish, squid, shellfish, carrion, seaweed

RANGE: surface-dweller, living mostly in southern parts of the Western Interior Seaway

Smaller than *Archelon*, but also a strong swimmer, *Protostega* had a lightweight framework of widely spaced bones covered by thick, leathery skin. While its rafter-like structure reduced *Protostega*'s weight and helped maximize its speed, it also made it open to attack by predators. A large exposed area between the head and body made it even more vulnerable. *Protostega* likely left the water to lay eggs on sandy beaches, similar to leatherback turtles of today.

TOXOCHELYS (TOKS-UH-KEE-LEEZ)

SIZE: up to 2 metres (6 feet) long **DIET**: seaweed, jellyfish, carrion

RANGE: bottom-dweller in shallow waters of the Western Interior Seaway

With its lightweight shell and boxy look, medium-sized *Toxochelys* resembled a modern leatherback turtle. Flattened wrist and ankle bones boosted its speed and power in the water, but they hampered movements on land. Judging from the high number of *Toxochelys* fossils discovered, it was one of the most abundant turtles in the Seaway. For mosasaurs and sharks, *Toxochelys* was likely an easy target. One mighty chomp of their strong jaws crunched through this smaller turtle's shell, rewarding these predators with a tasty meal.

SHARKS

Sharks first appeared around 400 million years ago and, for the most part, they have kept the same body shape and habits ever since. Sharks do not have a skeleton made of bone like other fish. Instead their skeletons are composed of cartilage, a flexible connective tissue. Cartilage decays at a faster rate than bone so fossils of sharks are rare. On occasion, fossilized vertebrae (centra) surface, but shark teeth are more common. Teeth are composed of tough enamel, and since sharks shed their teeth continuously through their lives, the Western Interior Seaway is peppered with fossil teeth from these predators.

Like sharks of today, sharks of the Late Cretaceous period had dual roles. They were hunters in search of their next meal, but they were also scavengers. By "recycling" dead animals, sharks cleaned the Seaway and helped maintain the ecosystem.

SQUALICORAX (SKWA-LIH-COR-AX)

NAME MEANS: crow shark

SIZE: up to 5 metres (16 feet) long

DIET: turtles, small mosasaurs, *Ichthyodectes*, other boney fish, and carrion

RANGE: coastlines of the Western Interior Seaway

Weighing in some cases as much as a grand piano, *Squalicorax* had a streamlined, muscular body shaped like a grey shark. Its jaw was filled with numerous sharp, heart-shaped, serrated teeth. *Squalicorax* satisfied its appetite by hunting down smaller prey but also attacked larger animals sometimes equal or greater in size to itself. Not a picky eater, it also consumed dead animals drifting past or lying on the bottom of the Seaway.

CRETOXYRHINA (CREH-TOX-EE-RYE-NAH)

NAME MEANS: Cretaceous jaws

SIZE: up to 7 metres (23 feet) long

DIET: fish, turtles, squid, mosasaurs, other sharks, carrion

RANGE: open water of the Western Interior Seaway

Nicknamed the "Ginsu shark" after a brand of kitchen knives that slice and dice, *Cretoxyrhina* was probably the largest and fiercest shark in the Western Interior Seaway. Razor-sharp, smooth teeth strengthened with thick enamel gave *Cretoxyrhina* the edge in battle. With mighty bites, *Cretoxyrhina* sheered through bone and tissue, sometimes losing teeth as it downed its prey. *Cretoxyrhina* teeth have been discovered embedded in bones of mosasaurs and large fish like *Xiphactinus*, proof that even the Seaway's top predators could be on its menu.

BATTLE OF THE GIANTS

Step right up for a seaside seat. Five oversized predators are poised to battle in the warm waters of the Western Interior Seaway. They're all fierce fighters. They all have unique strengths, as well as flaws. Most importantly, they're all hungry. It's anybody's guess who will win in this battle of the ages.

BEASTS OF THE WESTERN INTERIOR SEA!

ELASMOSAURUS

- Long neck with seventy-one vertebrae for an extra long reach
- Small head perched far from the body makes this fighter look deceptively small
- Mouthful of thin, spiked teeth to pierce and hold prey
- Four equal-sized, long, paddle-like flippers give powerful bursts of speed
- Broad, barrel-shaped body adds balance and buoyancy
- Up to 14 metres (46 feet) of steely muscle

FATAL FLAW: Like an overly wide raft, it's not easy to change course on a moment's notice.

BEASTS OF THE WESTERN INTERIOR SEA!

TYLOSAURUS

- Slender body streamlined for swimming
- Long tail, flattened laterally for powerful swishes
- Flipper-like fins with webbing between elongated bones to manoeuvre quickly
- Two rows of flanged teeth to grip and chomp prey
- Double-hinged jaw and flexible skull for an extra wide bite
- Up to 15 metres (49 feet) of hungry muscle

FATAL FLAW: Oversized chomp plus oversized appetite makes for a choking hazard.

ELASMOSAURUS

TYLOSAURUS

BEASTS OF THE
WESTERN INTERIOR SEA!

BEASTS OF THE
WESTERN INTERIOR SEA!
XIPHACTINUS

XIPHACTINUS

- A fearsome, bulldoggish head
- Sharp teeth in an upturned jaw to seize and puncture prey
- Forked tail and wing-like pectoral fins for smooth, speedy glides
- Streamlined shape to cut through the water
- Muscular body and a backbone of over 100 vertebrae for strength and agility
- Up to 6 metres (20 feet) long

FATAL FLAW: In a rush to eat everything and anything, it sometimes swallows more than it can handle, and dies after eating prey too large for its stomach.

BEASTS OF THE
WESTERN INTERIOR SEA!

CRETOXYRHINA

- Streamlined, muscular body for powerful, quick moves
- Immense jaw for wide bites
- Sharp, smooth teeth reinforced with strong enamel to slice and dice through bone and tissue
- Vicious hunter, not afraid to attack larger targets
- Up to 7 metres (23 feet) long

FATAL FLAW: Attacking prey that is similar in size and even larger than itself means that sometimes it becomes the prey.

CRETOXYRHINA

BEASTS OF THE
WESTERN INTERIOR SEA!

ARCHELON

- Wide flippers for powerful thrusts
- Sharp, pointed beak with a large overbite useful for cracking open hard shells
- Leathery covering over vaulted skeletal framework for buoyancy and lighter weight
- Up to 4 metres (13 feet) long, snout to tail

FATAL FLAW: Leathery covering offers little protection on land or in the sea.

ARCHELON

BIRDS

One of the greatest fossil discoveries of modern times was made in a limestone quarry near Solnhofen, Germany. Embedded in rock, paleontologists discovered the *Archaeopteryx*, a creature from the Late Jurassic period that looked like a perfect combination of bird and dinosaur. Like dinosaurs, *Archaeopteryx* had teeth, claws, and a long tail. Like birds, it had broad wings and flight feathers.

The discovery of *Archaeopteryx* sparked scientific debate. Did birds evolve from dinosaurs? Recently, other bird fossils with dinosaur features have been discovered, adding proof to the evolutionary argument.

During the Cretaceous period, bird evolution kicked into high gear. Along the Western Interior Seaway, several varieties populated the area. Some were like large penguins—flightless, awkward on land, but terrific swimmers. Others were more like seagulls—capable of flight, but shore-dwellers. Whatever their size or flight capabilities, birds fished the Seaway for prey, wary of predators like mosasaurs and crocodiles who found birds to be tasty mouthfuls.

HESPERORNIS (HES-PER-OR-NIS)

NAME MEANS: western bird

SIZE: up to 1.8 metres (6 feet) long

DIET: carnivorous; small fish

RANGE: lower shelf regions and northern shorelines of the Western Interior Seaway

The largest of the bird varieties found along the Western Interior Seaway, *Hesperornis* was a flightless bird but a masterful swimmer and diver. With kicks of its strong legs, it targeted fish underwater, changed direction and depth with its rudder-like tail and short wings, and snatched and held on to its prey with sharp teeth that locked into place when its jaws closed. Although fossils of *Hesperornis* have been found along the southern regions of the Seaway, most are from Canada, indicating that *Hesperornis* may have preferred cooler waters in northern regions.

Much like modern penguins, *Hesperornis* probably lived in colonies. They may have ventured onto land to lay eggs and raise young, and manoeuvred by awkwardly waddling or pushing themselves across rocks like seals. Being both aquatic and a land-dweller made *Hesperornis* a target for predators from both land and sea.

ICHTHYORNIS (IK-FEE-OR-NISS)

NAME MEANS: fish bird

SIZE: up to 30 cm (1 foot) long

DIET: fish

RANGE: shoreline of the Western Interior Seaway

Built for efficiency and long flights, *Ichthyornis* looked much like a seagull. With fused bones in its long wings and tail, *Ichthyornis* could make fine adjustments during flight and take advantage of prevailing air currents, allowing it to fly great distances for long periods. Swooping over the shallows, it scooped up unsuspecting fish near the surface, and pierced and held them in razor-sharp recurved teeth, making *Ichthyornis* a formidable predator along the shorelines of the Western Interior Seaway.

BAPTORNIS (BAP-TOR-NIS)

NAME MEANS: diving bird

SIZE: up to 1 metre (3.3 feet) long; similar to a loon **DIET**: fish

RANGE: shallows and shorelines of the Western Interior Seaway

Baptornis probably migrated to northern regions in the summer to breed, then returned to warmer southern areas when seasons changed. Heavy bones allowed *Baptornis* to dive and swim underwater. Using its wings to change direction and depth, its feet to push through the water and its long neck and tooth-lined beak to reach and grasp prey, *Baptornis* fished the Seaway, dining on smaller species like the sabre-toothed "herring," *Enchodus*. Because its lower legs were flush against its body and its feet pointed sideways, *Baptornis* was streamlined for swimming, but clumsy on land. Out of the water it probably hopped, waddled, or slid along rocks to move around.

CROCODILES

Although a rare find, crocodile fossils have been unearthed along the Western Interior Seaway, from Texas in the south to Wilson River, Manitoba in the north. These prehistoric crocodiles rested on shore and peninsulas, but hunted the shorelines, preying on animals like fish and seabirds. Compared to most crocodiles today, they were massive. Some measured over 7.6 metres (25 feet), a full person longer than today's largest crocodile—the saltwater species. Because crocodile fossils are so rare, especially in northern regions, scientists speculate that water temperatures might not have been warm enough for crocodiles to thrive. It's also possible that other reptiles like mosasaurs and plesiosaurs out-fished and out-hunted crocodiles, diminishing their food supply.

INVERTEBRATES

Long before the Western Interior Seaway existed, North America was covered by a large ocean and teemed with invertebrate life. However, after a number of extinction events, invertebrates gave way to vertebrates, though many survived into the Cretaceous period and even today.

SQUID: Squid living in the Western Interior Seaway could be enormous. One variety, *Tusoteuthis*, may have been 7.5 metres (25 feet) long. Being an invertebrate, *Tusoteuthis* lacked a boney framework. In place of a backbone, it had a gladius or pen, a hard structure of connective tissue in the region behind the head (mantle) that provided support for the animal. While fleshy parts decomposed, the gladius sometimes fossilized, giving paleontologists clues to the extinct creature's ways.

With eight arms and two tentacles, *Tusoteuthis* probably moved much like its modern relatives. By pulling water into the mantle, then pushing it out, *Tusoteuthis* created a kind of jet propulsion. Large eyes detected dim light and shadowy movement far below the surface. Hundreds of suction cups filled with hard, sharp, finely serrated tissue lined the insides of the arms and tentacles. Reaching out with its tentacles, *Tusoteuthis* caught its prey, held on fast with its sucker rings, drew the food toward its powerful beak, then ripped it to shreds before swallowing it.

CLAMS: Fossilized shells of *Inoceramus*, a giant clam, have been found along the Seaway, some as big around as inflatable swimming pools. Like modern clams, *Inoceramus* opened its shell to filter food from the water, but closed it when threatened to protect the fleshy parts inside. Some scientists believe the giant clam's oversized gills helped it to survive by giving it an efficient way of extracting oxygen from the oxygen-starved waters of the Western Interior Seaway.

AMMONITES: Ammonites are extinct, hard-shelled organisms whose living relatives are the squid and octopus of today. They moved by expelling water through a funnel-like opening and propelling themselves in the opposite direction. The smallest ammonites were the size of small buttons; the largest the size of tractor tires. An important food source in the Western Interior Seaway, smaller versions were tasty treats for large marine reptiles, which could scoop up thousands in a single gulp.

TRILOBYTES (BELOW) BECAME EXTINCT BEFORE THE TIME OF THE DINOSAURS, HOWEVER, MANY OTHER INVERTEBRATES SURVIVED.

DISCOVERIES EVERYWHERE

- In November 1988, Mike Trask and his twelve-year-old daughter Heather set out on a fossil hunt along Puntledge River in Courtenay, British Columbia. As they walked along, Mike drew chalk circles around potential fossils for Heather to excavate. While doing this, he noticed a cluster of odd-shaped rocks protruding from the shale ahead of him. Mike called Heather over and together they examined what Mike believed to be significant fossilized bones. Identification by the late Dr. Betsy Nicholls of the Royal Tyrrell Museum revealed their find was a record breaker—the first Elasmosaur discovered in British Columbia. Today, their discovery of the almost complete remains of the 80 million year old marine reptile is housed at the Courtenay and District Museum and Palaeontology Centre along with a replica of the complete skeleton.

- Road crews working on the Heartland Expressway near Gering, Nebraska cut into an ancient river channel and struck fossil pay dirt. Over a six-week period in 1999, paleontologists collected about 600 bones from the road construction site. Among the sixty species recovered: turtles, snakes, new species of beaver and gopher, three species of three-toed horses, and the sternum of a 2-metre-tall (6 feet) flightless bird. Paleontologists estimate that over the past five decades, more than 200,000 specimens have been saved from road construction sites, including a giant land tortoise and a plesiosaur from the Cretaceous period.

- In 2010, City of Edmonton workers Aaron Krywiak and Ryley Paul were jack-hammering a sewer tunnel nine storeys below ground when several interesting objects turned up in the rubble. One was a tooth. Later, crews discovered other bones. Police were called to see if the remains might be human. Identified as animal instead and possibly millions of years old, a paleontologist from the University of Alberta was then summoned to the excavation site. His conclusion: a tooth belonged to *Albertosaurus*, a relative of *T. Rex*, and a bone to *Edmontosaurus*, a hadrosaur. Although fossil bones frequently turn up in Alberta's soil, it was the first time sewer work yielded dinosaur remains.

- In 2000, when Doris Michaelson of Bellevue, Iowa read an article about a dinosaur discovery in the newspaper, she remembered an odd piece of bone that had been kicking around the house for decades and was sometimes used as a doorstop. Smooth, the size of a fist, it had been plucked from a conveyor in a gravel pit by her father in the 1930s. Curious about the bone, Michaelson contacted the Iowa Geological Survey and brought it to be identified. It proved to be a partially weathered 10 centimetre (4 inch) vertebra, likely from a hadrosaur.

- That same year, Michael Caldwell, a newly hired faculty member at the University of Alberta, discovered a forgotten treasure under a ping-pong table in the science lab. For decades, the table had been a work station where fossils were examined, but when Caldwell received money to renovate the lab, he decided to remove it. Tucked underneath the table, he found several boxes of marine reptile fossils that had been unearthed in Canada's Northwest Territories twenty-five years earlier. The bones belonged to four ichthyosaurs, two juveniles, and two adults, from a genus of ichthyosaur never discovered before. Inside one of the adults, Caldwell discovered two embryos, adding more proof that ichthyosaurs were livebearers.

- In an area of Minnesota that had been submerged under the Western Interior Seaway, a volunteer with the Science Museum of Minnesota discovered something more than shark teeth, clams, or ammonites. In 2015, after being hunched over for a few hours while digging at the former Hill Annex Mine, Len Jannusch got up to walk. A short distance away, he spotted an unusually shaped fragment sitting exposed near a deer trail. Curved and 4.5 centimetres (1.8 inches) long, it was a ninety-million-year-old claw. Based on its shape and size, paleontologists believe it belonged to a theropod, a two-legged carnivorous dinosaur, making it the first dinosaur fossil discovered in Minnesota.

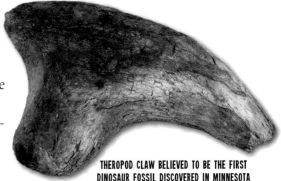

THEROPOD CLAW BELIEVED TO BE THE FIRST
DINOSAUR FOSSIL DISCOVERED IN MINNESOTA

GONE, BUT NOT COMPLETELY

WHAT HAPPENED SIXTY-SIX MILLION YEARS AGO?

Sixty-six million years ago, dinosaurs, marine reptiles, and many other life forms vanished. It's not as if they were alive one day and then gone the next. Whatever caused their extinction likely occurred over many thousands of years. Still, compared to the 185 million years that these creatures dominated the planet, it is but a tiny drop in the vast ocean of time.

What happened sixty-six million years ago? Scientists have been debating the reasons for one of the Earth's greatest extinctions for a long time. Three theories are popular.

VOLCANIC UPHEAVAL—Large volcanic eruptions around the globe unleashed waves of lava and released chlorine gas, sulfur dioxide, and carbon dioxide into the atmosphere. These poisoned the air and water and raised global temperatures. Unable to adapt to the catastrophic changes, many species died.

ASTEROID IMPACT—In 1980, American geologist Walter Alvarez discovered high levels of iridium in rock layers just above those containing dinosaur fossils. Although iridium is rare on Earth, asteroids and comets contain high concentrations of the metal. The discovery prompted another theory. Sixty-six million years ago, a massive iridium-rich asteroid speeding through space

plowed into the Earth, creating a huge impact
crater. The impact fired clouds of dust into the atmosphere, darkened the
sky, and blocked out the sun. Without sunlight, the Earth turned cold. Most plants died, and so, too, did many
animals—marine reptiles and dinosaurs included.

Evidence supporting the Alvarez theory was found in 1990 when scientists tested sixty-six-million-year-old
rock samples extracted from a giant crater discovered in the Chicxulub region of the Yucatán Peninsula. The
rocks contained high concentrations of shocked quartz grains and small glass beads known as tektites, materials
that typically form under explosive, extreme heat conditions, like those associated with asteroid impacts. The
Chicxulub impact crater is more than 180 kilometres (110 miles) across and 20 kilometres (12 miles) deep, making
it one of the largest impact structures on the planet. Judging from its size, scientists estimate that sixty-six million
years ago an asteroid at least 10 kilometres (6 miles) in diameter smashed into the Earth, setting off a wave of dust
and destruction.

ANTIPODAL VOLCANISM—A third theory connects the other two. Centuries of volcanic activity worsened after a
giant asteroid smashed into the planet. Impact waves reverberated through the ground, coming to their highest
concentration at a point on the Earth opposite to the impact crater in a region known as the antipode. Triggered by
massive shock waves, new fractures opened. Violent eruptions around the antipode followed, spewing a torrent of
lava and poisonous gases.

Support for the antipodal theory was bolstered by the discovery of a huge lava field in India that dates back to
the time Cretaceous creatures disappeared. Known as the Deccan Traps, it is on the other side of the planet from
the Chicxulub impact crater. Research shows that the Deccan Traps had three powerful eruption periods and
released 10,000 cubic kilometres (2400 cubic miles) of lava in less than a century.

PROTECTING THE PAST

Gone is the Western Interior Seaway. After the Cretaceous period, land rose, sea levels dropped, and the Seaway drained. Gone, too, are most of the Cretaceous creatures that lived in and around the Seaway. All we have left is the evidence of their existence: sedimentary deposits riddled with fossils.

In skilled hands, fossils speak for creatures who cannot speak for themselves. Like pieces of a giant puzzle, they tell the story of a time before human existence. But when fossils disappear or are mistreated, plucked out of the soil without care or analysis, pieces of the puzzle disappear, too.

In the 1890s, tree-trunk fossils from palm-like plants called cycads were discovered near the Black Hills of South Dakota. Thousands of specimens lay exposed on the ground. The site was one of the greatest concentrations of Cretaceous cycads in the world. In 1922, recognizing the need to preserve the fossils, U.S. President Warren G. Harding created Fossil Cycad National Monument. Located southwest of the town of Hot Springs, the site was the size of 260 soccer fields.

FOSSIL CYCAD
NATIONAL MONUMENT
1922 - 1957

© NPS

If you try to find Fossil Cycad National Monument today, you might have problems. After the creation of the park, cycad fossils disappeared, scooped off the surface by fossil hunters for scientific research, displays in museums, and private collections. Rare fossils of Cretaceous plants that flourished at the time of the dinosaurs vanished. Once stripped of its fossils, there was little to justify the park's existence. In 1957, the United States Congress de-authorized Fossil Cycad National Monument and removed it from the National Park system.

What happened to Fossil Cycad National Monument could easily happen in other places that are rich in fossils. Left unprotected and unregulated, their fossils could disappear, too. Without proper rules and procedures, the unbroken record of the past might be destroyed or vanish completely.

MODERN-DAY CYCADS
CLOSELY RESEEMBLE THEIR
PREHISTORIC ANCESTORS

EVERYDAY PEOPLE MAKE A DIFFERENCE

BONNER FAMILY—SMOKY HILL RIVER VALLEY, KANSAS

In 1925, Marion Bonner, a student at Wichita County High School, ventured into the badlands of western Kansas on a fossil-hunting excursion organized by his science teacher. Within hours of combing the chalk beds, he found a Cretaceous fish skull. Hooked on fossils from that moment, Marion read books on the subject, visited museums, consulted experts, and eventually became a member of the Society of Vertebrae Paleontology. His passion later spread to his wife, Margaret, and their eight children. Packed into the family's 1949 Chevy Suburban, they drove down bumpy roads into remote chalk beds to search for fossils. When Marion died in 1992, others in the family carried on the tradition.

After decades of fossil hunting, the Bonners amassed quite a record. They've excavated thousands of fossils, some of them unique or new to science. In 1987, Chuck Bonner discovered a short-necked plesiosaur with a fetus in the abdominal region. Nicknamed "Polly the Pregnant Plesiosaur," it was the first evidence that plesiosaurs were livebearers and not egg-layers.

GEORGE STERNBERG, LEFORD WENDELL, AND MARION BONNER

Many marine fossils unearthed by the Bonner family grace universities and natural history museums around North America. In 2010, the Bonner family received a special honour. An unusual filter fish discovered by the Bonners forty years earlier was identified as a new genus. To recognize the Bonner's many contributions to paleontology, it was named *Bonnerichthys gladius*.

PHOTO OF MARION BONNER (TOP CENTRE) AND CLASSMATES DURING A FOSSIL HUNTING FIELD TRIP WITH HIS SCHOOL

MARION BONNER, STEVE BONNER, AND GEORGE STERNBERG AT THE TURTLE QUARRY

DON BELL AND HENRY ISAAK—MORDEN, MANITOBA

While on a canoe trip in 1972, teachers Don Bell and Henry Isaak heard of a recent discovery of dinosaurs in the Morden area. The following weekend, the two investigated. Lying exposed in a field just west of Morden, they discovered a large fossil bone, not from a dinosaur but from a very large marine reptile. Ill-equipped to cart it home, they drove back to town to regroup. By the time they returned, two other men were at the site, hammering the fossil bone to pieces.

Realizing that miners from the Pembina Mountain Clays mining company frequently unearthed marine fossils, Bell and Isaak embarked on a mission to save as many as possible. They struck a deal with the miners. Whenever fossils surfaced, miners placed a call to the pair. In the evening, after the miners had shut down for the day, the two teachers salvaged what they could before operations resumed in the morning. Sometimes they worked through the night, excavating and jacketing fossils by the glow of headlights. They carted their prizes home and stored them in Henry's garage and Don's basement.

What started as a small-scale operation mushroomed. Interest spread. Volunteers, university students, and paleontologists joined the effort, and in just two years the team unearthed thirty mosasaurs, twenty plesiosaurs, and hundreds of other fossils. When the collection outgrew the basement and garage, it was transferred to the newly established Morden and District Museum. In 1979, it moved to other quarters in the lower level of Morden's Recreational Centre under a new name—the Canadian Fossil Discovery Centre.

Today, excavations continue around the fossil-rich Morden area and the collection continues to grow. The Canadian Fossil Discovery Centre now houses the largest number of marine vertebrates in Canada, thanks in part to Don Bell and Henry Isaak.

PHOTO LEFT TO RIGHT:
DAVE LUMGAIR, HENRY ISAAK, AND DON BELL
PADDLING TOGETHER THE DAY THEY LEARNED
"DINOSAUR" BONES HAD BEEN DISCOVERED
NEAR MORDEN, MB.

CLARENCE JOHNSRUD—TRENTON, NORTH DAKOTA

CLARENCE JOHNSRUD POSING WITH SOME OF HIS FOSSIL DISCOVERIES

In 1987, road crews rebuilding a highway near Trenton, North Dakota, unearthed beautifully preserved plant fossils in the upturned stone. Forced by changing weather and a tight budget, road crews couldn't afford to stop and save the fossils.

DAWN REDWOOD FOSSIL

When Clarence Johnsrud, a local sugar-beet farmer, heard of the discovery, he negotiated an arrangement with the road supervisor to allow him a few days to haul away as much stone as possible before crews buried the rest under the new road. With hand tools, Clarence broke large slabs into pieces, loaded them into his truck, brought them home, and stored them in his barn. Over the next few years, using a hammer and chisel, he split some 20 tons of rock and recovered hundreds of delicate leaf fossils from the Paleocene age (fifty-eight million years ago). Today, Clarence Johnsrud's leaf fossils are on display in museums across the country, from North Dakota's Heritage Center in Bismark, to Denver's Museum of Natural History, and the Florida Natural History Museum in Gainesville.

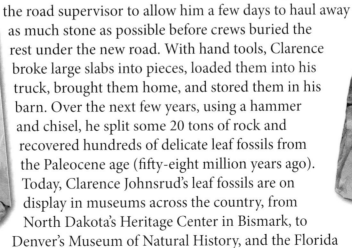

SYCAMORE FOSSIL

HORSE CHESTNUT FOSSIL

FOSSIL-HUNTING GUIDELINES

Most provinces and states have laws that govern fossil hunting. Often the laws differ from region to region. In some places, collecting and selling fossils is legal. In others, it is against the law to dig for or even pick up fossils. In still others, it is legal, but only on private property and with the permission of the landowner.

For example, in Alberta you cannot hunt for fossils in parks and other protected areas, but you can collect surface fossils from privately owned property as long as you have permission from the landowner. You cannot excavate for them, however, and whatever you find legally belongs to the Province of Alberta.

In Manitoba, the rules are different. Fossils are heritage objects, protected and owned by the province. To excavate vertebrate fossils, a qualified individual or organization needs to apply for a permit from the province and have the consent of the landowner before they can begin.

Before embarking on any fossil hunt, research the laws for your region. Respect and obey the rules and regulations. Treat each fossil as a treasured piece of information, a part of the giant puzzle that is our prehistory.

WHAT TO DO IF YOU FIND A FOSSIL

If you spot a fossil, leave it as you found it. To help authorities locate the fossil:

- Photograph it. If possible, include a recognizable object in the photo to give an idea of the fossil's scale.

- Record the fossil's location on a map or note its GPS coordinates. Take pictures of the surroundings and record the locations of prominent features in the area. The more detail you can provide authorities, the easier it will be for them to find the fossil.

- Contact your local museum to report your find. Make arrangements to provide authorities with your photographs and the other information you've collected.

HOW TO GET INVOLVED

VOLUNTEER

Working side-by-side with skilled professionals can give you valuable training in the ways of paleontology. At the Canadian Fossil Discovery Centre, for example, there are a number of dig options, from single-day experiences to week-long excursions. Contact museums and paleontological societies in your area or check their websites for information about how you can get involved in ongoing digs.

DIG FOR INFORMATION

Check the magazine racks of a bookstore or your local library for titles such as *Prehistoric Times*, *Canadian Geographic*, *National Geographic*, *Smithsonian* magazine, *EARTH* magazine, and *Discover* magazine. Most feature discovery stories and the latest news from dig sites around the world. Many of these print publications also have online versions that allow you to search through archives for past issues and subjects that interest you.

VISIT

Many museums and science centres along the Western Interior Seaway—like the ones listed on the following pages—display marine reptile and dinosaur fossils. When you travel, stop for a visit. Check out exhibits and program options.

CANADIAN
FOSSIL
DISCOVERY
CENTRE

WHERE TO SEE CRETACEOUS FOSSILS ALONG THE WESTERN INTERIOR SEAWAY

CANADIAN FOSSIL DISCOVERY CENTRE

Morden, Manitoba

Visit the largest collection of Cretaceous marine reptiles in Canada and participate in digs along the Manitoba Escarpment.

Five-star sampler: Impressive "Bruce," the world's largest displayed mosasaur and the official fossil emblem of Manitoba.

Website: www.discoverfossils.com

ROYAL TYRRELL MUSEUM

Drumheller, Alberta

Relive the ancient past with dig programs and ten galleries devoted to paleontology.

Five-star sampler: *Shonisaurus sikanniensis*, a 21-metre-long ichthyosaur that is the world's largest marine reptile.

Website: www.tyrrellmuseum.com

T.REX DISCOVERY CENTRE

Eastend, Saskatchewan

Take a closer look at Saskatchewan's dinosaurs, marine reptiles, and prehistoric mammals.

Five-star sampler: "Scotty," a *Tyrannosaurus rex* discovered in the Eastend region.

Website: www.royalsaskmuseum.ca

THE ED LEITH CRETACEOUS MENAGERIE

Wallace Building, University of Manitoba
Winnipeg, Manitoba

Learn about Manitoba's Cretaceous period through its rocks and fossils.

Five-star sampler: Giant *Archelon* dangling from the ceiling.

Website: www.umanitoba.ca/geoscience/cretaceousmenagerie

STERNBERG MUSEUM OF NATURAL HISTORY

Hays, Kansas

Discover the marine reptiles that once swam over Kansas and much more including the third-largest collection of pterosaurs in the world.

Five-star sampler: George F. Sternberg's famous "fish-within-a-fish": a 2 metre (6 feet) *Gillicus* inside a 4 metre (14 feet) *Xiphactinus*.

Website: www.sternberg.fhsu.edu

SAM NOBLE OKLAHOMA MUSEUM OF NATURAL HISTORY

University of Oklahoma
Norman, Oklahoma

Investigate Oklahoma's prehistory through models, specimens, and interactive stations in the Hall of Ancient Life.

Five-star sampler: "Clash of the Titans" exhibit, where the world's largest *Apatosaurus* squares off against *Saurophaganax*.

Website: www.samnoblemuseum.ou.edu

FORT WORTH MUSEUM OF SCIENCE AND HISTORY

Fort Worth, Texas

Explore Texas dinosaurs through exhibits and activities in the Dinolabs and Dinodig galleries.

Five-star sampler: 18 metre (60 feet) *Paluxysaurus*, the State Dinosaur of Texas.

Website: www.fwmuseum.org

GLOSSARY

ABSOLUTE DATING—determining the actual age or age range of a fossil or rock using chemical or physical tests.

AGE OF REPTILES—the period about 252 million years ago to about 66 million years ago when dinosaurs and marine reptiles thrived.

AMMONITES—extinct organisms with coiled, multi-chambered shells that were especially abundant in the Mesozoic age.

BENTONITE—a mineral composed of ancient compressed volcanic ash.

CARNIVORE—an animal that feeds on flesh.

CARRION—dead and decaying flesh.

CHALK—soft, white, porous sedimentary rock composed of calcium carbonate.

CHEVRON—one of a series of triangle-shaped bones on the underside of the tail in many reptiles.

CONSOLIDANT—a hardening solution applied to a specimen to give it strength.

CONVECTION—the circular movement in a fluid caused by an uneven distribution of heat.

CT SCAN—a three-dimensional image of a cross section of tissue or bone that is made with X-rays.

CYCAD—a type of evergreen plant with palm-like leaves that lives in tropical and subtropical regions.

DECOMPOSE—to break down organic matter into simpler components or chemical parts.

DNA—a substance in the cells of plants and animals that carries genetic information.

ERA—a major division of geological time that is usually divided into smaller units called periods.

ESCARPMENT—a long, steep slope that separates areas of land at different heights.

FIELD JACKET—an outer covering of plaster that is wrapped around a fossil to protect it before it is moved from the site where it was discovered.

GENUS—a group of related plants or animals.

GEOLOGIST—a scientist who studies the Earth and its formations.

GLADIUS—the internal skeleton of the squid.

HALF-LIFE—the amount of time it takes for half of the atoms in a radioactive material to decay.

HERBIVORE—an animal that feeds on plants.

IN SITU—"on site" or "in position"; in paleontology, in situ refers to a fossil that has not been moved from the site where it was discovered.

INVERTEBRATE—animals lacking backbones such as insects and worms.

LATE CRETACEOUS PERIOD—a segment of geological time 136 to 66 million years ago.

MATRIX—the solid matter in which a fossil is embedded.

OMNIVORE—an animal that eats both plants and other animals.

OVERBURDEN—the material covering a fossil, mineral, or rock deposit.

PALEOARTIST—an artist who depicts subjects related to paleontology.

PALEONTOLOGIST—a scientist who finds, studies, and interprets fossil evidence from prehistoric times.

PANGAEA—a supercontinent of all the Earth's landmasses that is thought to have existed before the Triassic period.

PANTHALASSA—the vast ocean that once surrounded the supercontinent Pangaea.

PERIOD—a division of geological time smaller than an era during which a single type of rock system is formed.

PLANKTON—very tiny plant and animal organisms such as microscopic diatoms and algae that float or drift in the water.

RELATIVE DATING—determining the approximate age of a fossil or rock by comparing it to other fossils or rocks found at the same site.

REPLICA—an exact copy or model of something.

SCAVENGER—an animal that feeds on dead or decaying matter.

SEDIMENT—silt, sand, rocks, fossils, and other matter carried and deposited by water, wind, or ice.

SHALE—a fine-grained sedimentary rock usually red, green, grey, or black in colour consisting of compressed and hardened clay, silt, or mud.

SPECIES—an animal, plant, or other living thing that has distinctive features or characteristics from others in its group or genus.

STRATA—layers into which sedimentary rocks are divided.

UNDERCUT—to cut away rock from the underside of a fossil in order to leave an overhanging portion.

VERTEBRATE—animals with backbones such as mammals, birds, fish, reptiles, and amphibians.

SELECTED REFERENCES

BOOKS

Calaway, Jack M., and Elizabeth L. Nicholls, eds. *Ancient Marine Reptiles*. San Diego: Academic Press, 1997.

Eldredge, Niles. *Extinction and Evolution: What Fossils Reveal About the History of Life*. Buffalo, NY: Firefly Books, 2014.

Ellis, Richard. *Sea Dragons: Predators of the Prehistoric Oceans*. Lawrence, KS: University Press of Kansas, 2003.

Everhart, Michael. *Sea Monsters: Prehistoric Creatures of the Deep*. Washington, DC: National Geographic, 2007.

Fortey, Richard. *Fossils: The Key to the Past*. Washington, DC: Smithsonian Institution Press, 2002.

Huck, Barbara. *In Search of Canada's Ancient Heartland: Discover Manitoba's Geology, Paleontology and Archaeology*. Winnipeg: Heartland Associates, 2015.

Lambert, David. *Encyclopedia of Prehistory*. New York: Facts on File, 2002.

Marvin, Nigel, and Jasper James. *Chased by Sea Monsters: Prehistoric Predators of the Deep*. London: BBC Books, 2003.

Palmer, Douglas. *Atlas of the Prehistoric World*. New York: Discovery Books, 1999.

Prehistoric Life: The Definitive Visual History of Life on Earth. New York: DK Publications, 2009.

BOOKS FOR YOUNG PEOPLE

Berkowitz, Jacob. *Jurassic Poop: What Dinosaurs (and others) Left Behind*. Toronto: Kids Can Press, 2006.

Brewster, Hugh. *Dinosaurs in Your Back Yard: The Coolest, Scariest Creatures Ever Found in the USA*. New York: Abrams Books for Young Readers, 2009.

Brown, Don. *Rare Treasure: Mary Anning and her Remarkable Discoveries*. Boston: Houghton Mifflin, 1999.

Camper, Cathy. *Bugs Before Time: Prehistoric Insects and their Relatives*. New York: Simon & Schuster Books for Young People, 2002.

Cumba, Stephen. *Sea Monsters*. Toronto: Kids Can Press, 2007.

Dixon, Dougal. *Prehistoric Life*. New York: Oxford University Press, 1993.

Walker, Sally. *Fossil Fish Found Alive: Discovering the Coelacanth*. Minneapolis: Carolrhoda Books, 2002.

WEBSITES

Canadian Fossil Discovery Centre. http://www.discoverfossils.com/.

Canadian Museum of Nature. Fossil Gallery. http://nature.ca/en/plan-your-visit/what-see-do/our-exhibitions/talisman-energy-fossil-gallery.

Everhart, Mike. Oceans of Kansas Paleontology. http://oceansofkansas.com/.

Live Science. Cretaceous Period: Animals, Plants and Extinction Event. http://www.livescience.com/29231-cretaceous-period.html.

Morden Museum. Ancient Seas of Manitoba. http://www.collectionscanada.gc.ca/eppp-archive/100/205/301/ic/cdc/ancientseas/uppercret.htm.

National Geographic. Prehistoric Animals. http://animals.nationalgeographic.com/animals/prehistoric/.

Smithsonian National Museum of Natural History. Dinosaurs in Your Back Yard. http://naturalhistory.si.edu/exhibits/backyard-dinosaurs/.

University of Manitoba. The Ed Leith Cretaceous Menagerie. http://umanitoba.ca/geoscience/cretaceousmenagerie/welcome.htm.

ONLINE MAGAZINES WITH ARTICLES ABOUT PALEONTOLOGY AND PREHISTORY

Discover Magazine. http://discovermagazine.com/tags/paleontology.

EARTH. http://www.earthmagazine.org/tags/paleontology.

National Geographic. http://www.nationalgeographic.com/search?proxystylesheet=site_search&output=xml_no_dtd&site=site_search&client=site_search&getfields=*&requiredfields=description&q=paleontology.

Natural History. http://www.naturalhistorymag.com/topics/dinosaurs.

Science. http://www.sciencemag.org/category/paleontology.

Scientific American. http://www.scientificamerican.com/archaeology-and-paleontology/.

The Scientist. http://www.the-scientist.com/?articles.list/tagNo/25/tags/paleontology/.

Smithsonian Magazine. http://www.smithsonianmag.com/tag/paleontology/?no-ist.

PHOTO, MAP, AND IMAGE CREDITS

The author and publisher gratefully acknowledge the following for permission to reprint photographs, maps, and images for this book. Copyright holders and page numbers are listed below. Photos, maps, and images may not be reproduced without permission.

PHOTOS AND IMAGES

Pages 2–3: Wheat and Pea fields © Tyler Olson, www.Shutterstock.com #5559490; *Albertonectes* © Julius T. Csotonyi; *Xiphactinus* © Julius T. Csotonyi; Girl standing in the cave © Dmytro Vietrov, www.Shutterstock.com #302732270

Pages 4–5: Erupting volcano © Niyazz, www.Shutterstock.com #133742654; Gneiss © www.sandatlas.org, www.Shutterstock.com #137246309; Red granite and Sandstone © aleks-p, www.Shutterstock.com # 353357510, 353337563

Pages 8–9: Early Permian landscape © Julius T. Csotonyi

Page 10: *Clidastes* giving birth © Julius T. Csotonyi

Page 11: Illustration of *Massospondylus* dinosaurs in landscape; Julius T. Csotonyi; used with permission of the Royal Ontario Museum © ROM.

Page 12: Planet earth core © Solcan Sergiu, www.Shutterstock.com #350577647

Page 13: *Hesperonychus elizabethae* © Julius T. Csotonyi

Page 14: Engraving by G. R. Levillaire, *Histoire naturelle de la montagne de Saint-Pierre de Maestricht*, https://commons.wikimedia.org/wiki/File:MosasaurDiscovery.jpg, public domain; Mary Anning *Plesiosaurus* letter, https://commons.wikimedia.org/wiki/File:Mary_Anning_Plesiosaurus.jpg, public domain; Marjorie Courtenay-Latimer and Coelacanth, https://commons.wikimedia.org/wiki/File:Marjorie_Courtenay-Latimer_and_Coelacanth.jpg, licenced under the creative commons attribution share-alike from The South African Institute for Aquatic Biology (SAIAB, www.saiab.ac.za)

Page 15: Fish-within-a-Fish, image courtesy of Fort Hays State University's Sternberg Museum of Natural History; Skull of "Bruce" the Mosasaur used with permission of the Canadian Fossil Discovery Centre; Gas can © Kitch Bain, www.Shutterstock.com #61477366; Diatomaceous earth © Mona Makela, www.Shutterstock.com #128711975; Amber bracelet © Irena Misevic, www.Shutterstock.com #80194204

Pages 16–17: Dig site used with permission of the Canadian Fossil Discovery Centre; Crime scene tape © fredex, www.Shutterstock.com #272278520

Pages 18–19: *Lythronax* and *Squalicorax* © Julius T. Csotonyi

Page 20: True form fossil of *Trinacromerum* flipper used with permission of the Canadian Fossil Discovery Centre; Plant Leaf fossil © alice-photo, www.Shutterstock.com #164319647

Page 21: Gnat in amber © Bjoern Wylezich, www.Shutterstock.com #356778602; Ammonite mold and cast © ribeiroantonio, www.Shutterstock.com #52797868; Amber stones background © torook, www.Shutterstock.com #379813549

Page 22: *Tylosaurus* vertebrae; *Tylosaurus*, *Xiphactinus* and plesiosaur teeth used with permission of the Canadian Fossil Discovery Centre; Dinosaur Eggs © Jaroslav Moravcik, www.Shutterstock.com #239039095; Footprints in mud © Terence Walsh, www.Shutterstock.com #1214951

Page 24: Shale Rock © Dana283, www.Shutterstock.com #383317420; Chalk Cliff © Chris Pole, www.Shutterstock.com #204255589; Folded shale and bentonite used with permission of the Canadian Fossil Discovery Centre

Pages 26–27: "Bruce" the Mosasaur replica used with permission of the Canadian Fossil Discovery Centre

Pages 28–29: Exposed and tagged dig site, dig site grid, plesiosaur excavation, field jacket, matrix removal, and catalogued fossils used with permission of the Canadian Fossil Discovery Centre

Pages 30–31: Reconstruction of "Bruce" the Mosasaur sequence used with permission of the Canadian Fossil Discovery Centre

Pages 32–33: *Trincromerum* replica, *Clidastes* skull, *Hesperornis* skeleton, *Terminonaris* limb replica, and *Hesperornis lumgairi* bones used with permission of the Canadian Fossil Discovery Centre

Pages 34–35: Microscope, catalogued specimens, shelves of specimen drawers, *Clidastes* mold, fossils undergoing reconstruction, *Tylosaurus* tooth molds, and shelves of unopened field jackets used with permission of the Canadian Fossil Discovery Centre

Page 36: Layers of ground on cliff side © Fedor A. Sidorov, www.Shutterstock.com #2082752

Pages 37–38: Old yellowish paper © val lawless, www.Shutterstock.com #108100877

INDEX